Gardening
Month-by-Month

Gardening
Month~by~Month
PERCY THROWER

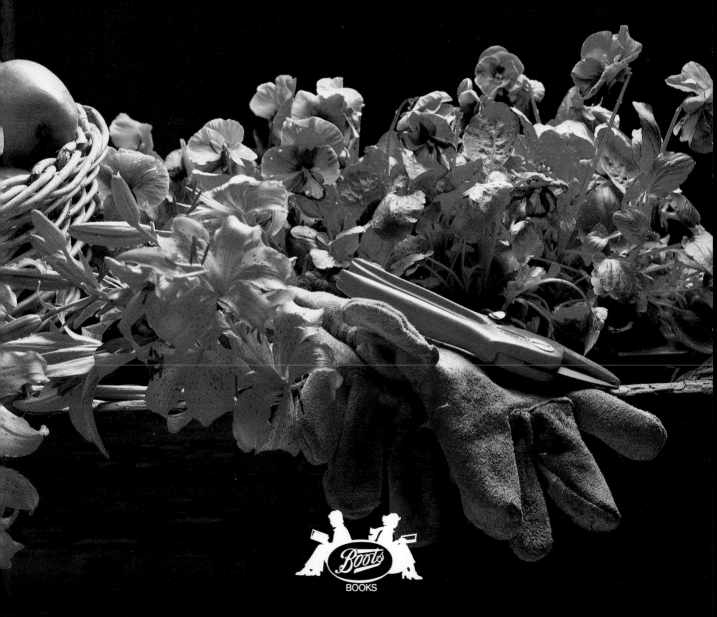

Boots
BOOKS

The publishers would like to thank the following for
supplying colour photographs: Pat Brindley, Valerie
Finnis, The Harry Smith Horticultural Collection,
Michael Warren, Zefa – London.

The endpapers show a range of gardening tools
available from the larger branches of Boots.

Illustrations by Stuart Perry

Photographs on cover, endpapers and title page by
Paul Williams.

Published for The Boots Company Limited by
The Hamlyn Publishing Group Limited
London · New York · Sydney · Toronto
Astronaut House, Feltham, Middlesex, England
Copyright © The Hamlyn Publishing Group
Limited 1980

Phototypeset in England by Tradespools Limited
in 11 on 12pt Apollo
Printed and bound in Spain
by Graficromo, S. A. – Córdoba

ISBN 0 600 37254 5

Contents

Introduction *10*

January *18*   July *70*

February *26*   August *78*

March *34*   September *86*

April *42*   October *94*

May *50*   November *102*

June *58*   December *110*

Vegetable sowing and harvesting chart *116*

Glossary of terms *118*

Index *121*

List of chemicals and suppliers *125*

Introduction

The Essentials of a Garden
Soils and Fertilisers
Growing Vegetables and Fruit
Using Chemicals
The Greenhouse

One of the secrets behind what makes a successful gardener is doing the right job at the right time. In putting together this month-by-month guide, I have tried to offer all gardeners a plan of campaign to cover the most important jobs in the gardening year.

However, it is important to remember that the time for doing certain tasks varies for different parts of the country, and will vary from year to year with the idiosyncrasies and vagaries of our climate. I have tried here to give the average: growing conditions may well be a fortnight advanced on this in the South and West, and anything from ten days to a fortnight later in the North. Spring may come early one year and very late the following one; so in all things you must be guided by the condition of the soil and the temperature, and take account of what is happening to the trees and plants around you when planning any major task.

The majority of gardeners nowadays, and here I speak for myself too, have to cope with the garden at weekends only throughout most of the year, and this does tend to limit the amount of work which can be done. We all have our favourite jobs, and those we are not so

keen on doing, so before any weekend it is necessary to decide what the essential jobs are and to then do these first. Otherwise it is all too easy to spend the time fiddling around and then find that the time has gone, the light has faded, and that the essential piece of digging, or whatever, has not been done. If we do plan ahead, gardening is easier and the garden is better as a result.

THE ESSENTIALS OF A GARDEN

When asked what are the bare essentials for any garden, I would answer a lawn, some shrubs, a tree if you have room, roses, some hardy border plants and some bulbs. If you have time, then bedding plants will add colour and interest to the basic mix throughout the summer months. What is important is not to cram too much into a small space, this

only makes every job more difficult and gives the garden a cluttered uncomfortable feel.

A GARDEN FROM SCRATCH

For many people these days, garden-making begins with a rough site left by a builder. My advice on how to cope with this is first to clear the area of all debris left by the builders, putting any stones and bricks on one side for path-making, and then get rid of the rest. Next, the whole area must be dug, and it may well be a good idea either to hire a cultivator to make the job easier, or get a contractor in to do it for you. Unless the soil is in very good condition, it would be advisable at this stage to work in as much organic matter (see page 13) as you are able to get hold of. This improves the soil texture and gets everything off to a better start.

Having cleared and dug the site, I would then grass the entire area. This will give you something pleasant to look at, and give the children somewhere to play while you can plan at leisure where to lay paths, plant trees and put the flower beds and vegetable plot. It is then a simple matter to dig in the grass where necessary and plant up gradually.

To help in selecting a range of plants which will give you

Introduction

colour and interest throughout the year, I have included under each month some of my own favourites which are likely to be looking good at that time of year. These have been arranged in alphabetical order using their botanical names as this will make it easier to find the plants listed both in garden centres and catalogues.

SOILS AND FERTILISERS

I think it would be helpful at this point to say something about the different types of soil. Soil affects all aspects of gardening: so much depends on it, that it is well worthwhile to spend some time studying it in order to determine what sort of treatment is needed to make it into the best possible growing medium.

Soils vary considerably, some dry out quickly, others get waterlogged, are sticky and heavy, or stoney. But basically, most soils are of two main types: light or heavy. A light soil will not stick in lumps and does not hold water easily. It has the advantages of being easily worked, and good for seed raising and growing flowers. It also makes a good winter garden and warms up more quickly in spring to give early vegetable crops.

A heavy soil holds moisture well, forms in lumps, sticks to shoes and tools, and sets to concrete in dry weather. It does, however, retain both moisture and plant foods better than a light soil, and so is potentially more fertile and, when well conditioned, is especially good for growing roses, fruits and vegetables.

Garden tools

The first essentials are a spade, fork, rake and hoe. Spades and forks are made in several sizes, so check the length and weight— remember you may be using them for several hours at a time.

Next to be acquired are a trowel, sharp knife, secateurs and shears. Then gradually you should get a watering can, wheelbarrow, spray equipment, lawn mower and hose which, incidentally, will stay in better condition if kept on a hose reel.

There are many other tools designed to do specific jobs but the ones listed here will get you off to a good start.

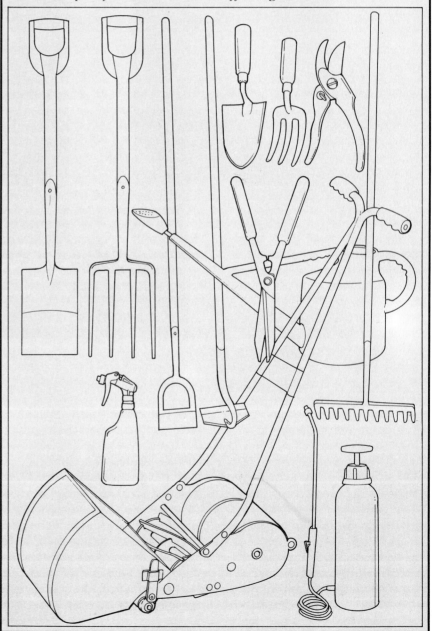

Soils which are intermediate between the two are the ideal. These are likely to be the result of good cultivation.

Improving the texture For improving both light and heavy soils, the basic requirements are the same: digging and the incorporation of some form of organic material such as garden compost, manure, spent hops, mushroom compost or peat. The organic material eventually gets broken down to a substance called humus, which has the effect of making a heavy soil more porous and easily worked, as well as improving the moisture-holding capacity of light soils.

Digging on heavy soils is always more beneficial if it can be done in late autumn, so that the soil is left in lumps, exposed to the action of the weather throughout the winter.

Acid or alkaline It is also important to find out whether the soil is acid or alkaline (chalky), as this affects the kind of plants which can be grown.

Acid soils, which are often also sandy or peaty in texture, are good for azaleas, rhododendrons, heathers, camellias and all related plants. Though the acidity can be lessened by the application of lime, it cannot be altered to any marked degree.

Alkaline soils generally occur in areas where the subsoil is of chalk or limestone, and are usually hungry soils as the plant foods are washed through so easily. There is a range of chalk-loving plants which includes the garden pinks and clematis.

Soil-testing kits are available which are easy to use and show not only if the soil is acid or alkaline but also to what degree. Also, other gardeners or garden centres in the neighbourhood will probably be able to give advice. Many soils, in fact, are neutral—neither acid nor alkaline—and these will grow a complete range of plants.

Fertilisers A plant uses sunlight, carbon dioxide from the air, moisture from the soil and various chemical elements to manufacture the food it needs for growth. The chemicals required must always be taken up, dissolved in water, either through the roots or, applied as foliar feeds, through the leaves. Plant roots, however, need air and moisture to function effectively. Without air they decay and die and this is likely to be the cause of plants failing in waterlogged soils or over-watered pots.

The three most important chemicals needed for plant growth are nitrogen, phos-phorus, and potassium (potash). These are often referred to by the symbols N, P and K respectively. In addition, other chemicals, the most important of which are manganese, magnesium and iron, are required in minute quantities.

Each chemical has a different effect on the growth of the plant. Nitrogen is used to promote fast growth and healthy green leaves, phos-phorus encourages good root growth and the formation of flowers, potash also encourages flower production and the ripening of fruits, as well as acting as a general tonic. As too much of one of these chemicals can sometimes be injurious, it is important that all three are applied in a balanced amount. This is best done by the use of a general garden fertiliser which can be either an inorganic one such as Growmore or an organic one such as blood, fish and bone.

The organic fertiliser is slower acting than the inorganic, and should be dug in some time in advance of planting. Inorganic fertilisers are quick acting and are sprinkled on the soil around the plant, after planting or during growth.

GROWING VEGETABLES AND FRUIT

In all but the smallest of gardens I think it well worthwhile to grow a selection of salad vegetables and some beans, spinach, cabbage and broccoli.

Apple and pear trees can be easily accommodated when grown as cordons or trained as espaliers against a wall or fence, and a blackberry makes a useful covering for a north-facing fence. Strawberries can be grown in a barrel on the patio.

Vegetables When growing vegetables the important thing to aim for is a continuity of cropping. For many crops—the salads, carrots, beetroots, peas and spinach—sowing little and often is the golden rule. A couple of yards of row at a time will give sufficient for eating, and not leave you with a glut or a lot of vegetables running up to seed.

In order to make the most of the vegetable plot I do recom-mend the use of cloches. These will enable you to get the soil into condition for earlier sowing, and to bring crops into cropping several weeks in advance of their normal period, and this is where the saving in money comes. Continuity in the case of some of the vegetables depends on growing a particular type at a particular time of the year. Advice on this is given in the table on page 116.

One point to remember when making outdoor sowings of most of the brassica crops, and this includes broccoli, Brussels sprouts, all the cabbages and cauliflowers, is that the seeds must be sown in a separate seedbed and transplanted into the cropping positions when the young plants are big enough to handle. This means that, not only are the sturdiest seedlings transplanted, but in the meantime the area can be used for quick-maturing crops such as lettuce, radish and peas.

Fruit In popularity for growing, I would put fruit in the following order: strawberries, raspberries, blackcurrants, gooseberries, apples, plums, pears, blackberries, loganberries, and then the remaining stone fruit—cherries, peaches, apricots and nectarines.

The growing of peaches, apricots and nectarines is never all that satisfactory in this country unless they can be grown under glass and I have not dealt with them in this book. Similarly, the only kind of cherry which is advisable to grow in a small garden is the Morello as a fan-trained specimen which can be protected from the birds. All other cherry trees grow too large to be netted effectively, so their potential crops are lost to the birds.

The best types of fruit trees for the average garden are apples and pears planted as bush trees on dwarfing rootstocks, or as cordons. For fan-training on walls there are pears, plums and apples for east- and west-facing walls and Morello cherry, blackberry and loganberry for north-facing walls.

Planting distances Bush trees on dwarfing rootstocks require a distance of 2·5 to 3 m (8 to 10 ft), cordons 1 m (3 ft) and fan-trained 4·5 m (15 ft) or more. Strawberries need to be 45 cm (18 in) apart with 60 cm (2 ft) between rows, raspberries 45 cm (18 in) apart, blackcurrants 1·5 m (5 ft) apart, gooseberries 1.25 m (4 ft) apart

and blackberries and loganberries 3 to 3·5 m (10 to 12 ft) apart.

Rootstocks Most of the top or tree fruit varieties cannot be grown successfully on their own roots. They are, therefore, grafted or budded onto a rootstock. The rootstock affects the ultimate height of the tree and also when it will start cropping. For the small garden, or when growing fruit as cordons, it is important to buy them grafted on to dwarfing rootstocks.

Pollination This is the term used for the transference of pollen from the male to the female parts of the flower which results in the formation of fruits or seeds. Pollination is especially important for fruit trees if they

are to crop satisfactorily.

Many plants can pollinate themselves and are known as self-fertile, but others are self-sterile and need to be cross pollinated from a similar plant. Many apples, pears, plums and cherries are self-sterile and must be pollinated with pollen from a compatible variety. Fruit trees grown in an adjoining garden and flowering at the same time may well fulfil this requirement, but otherwise it will be necessary to plant your own pollinators, and this must be taken into account when planning the number and type of trees you plant.

Growing in containers For use on the patio or terrace, apples, pears, plums, peaches

nectarines can all be grown in containers of a minimum size of 38 cm (15 in) in diameter and 25 to 30 cm (10 to 12 in) in depth. Use John Innes potting compost No. 3 and choose trees on a dwarfing rootstock. During the summer months the trees will need plenty of water and feeding with liquid fertiliser at frequent intervals. Such trees require little pruning and, other than cutting out diseased or overcrowded branches, summer pruning (page 84) will be sufficient.

THE USE OF CHEMICALS

Although I do not like to advocate an overuse of chemicals, I am a great believer in prevention being better than cure. Consequently I like to keep an eye on all the plants in the garden and greenhouse, and applying an insecticide or fungicide at the first sign of trouble or, in the case of diseases such as rose mildew, before there are any such signs. An insecticide against greenfly applied early in the year, say April or May, will do much to kill the pest before it has a chance to multiply and build up. Once the warmer, drier weather arrives, greenfly increase at such a rate you are unlikely to be able to keep up with them.

Used properly, garden chemicals do the job they are supposed to do, but if not used properly they do damage, and time and money will be wasted.

When applying chemical sprays, I cannot stress too much the need to follow the maker's instructions. Not to do so is folly and may cause

Introduction

damage to the plants as well as being dangerous to yourself. It is of particular importance to observe the specified intervals between the spraying and harvesting of fruit and vegetables crops.

Do all spraying in the evening to avoid harming bees, and make sure the containers of chemicals are stored well out of the reach of children. All spraying equipment should be well washed after use and empty chemical containers disposed of carefully. When spraying choose a still, dry day so that there will be no drifting on to other plants.

Chemicals available   There is a wide assortment of chemical sprays on the market. Many contain the same active ingredient, but differ in their trade names. All the insecticides and fungicides can be divided into two groups, the systemics or non-systemics, according to the way in which they work.

Systemic sprays are absorbed into the plant sap and are carried round to all parts of the plant. They remain effective for several weeks and will kill fungal diseases growing through the plant tissues, or insects feeding on any part of the plant.

Non-systemic sprays remain on the surface of the plant and affect the insect or disease by direct contact or by poisoning the surface of the plant. They are quickly washed off by rain and their application must therefore be repeated frequently.

Spraying equipment   There are many sorts of sprayer available; choose one which has

Greenhouses and frames

There are so many kinds of greenhouses available, that the choice is rather bewildering but whichever you choose it must have an open, sheltered position with plenty of light available.

With or without a greenhouse, it is worth investing in a garden frame as this provides space for plants and seedlings which do not require full greenhouse protection. The glass covering the frame is known as a light.

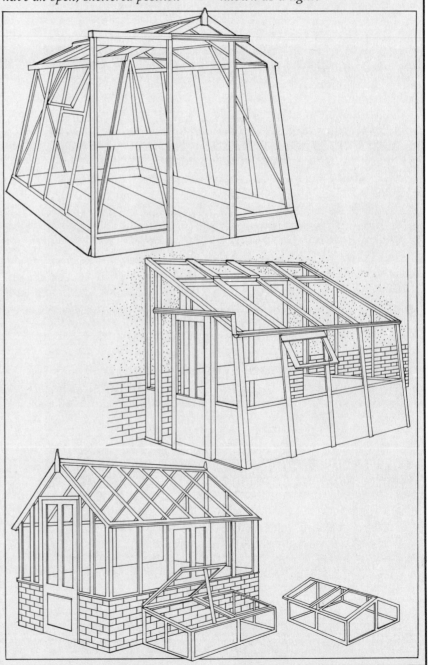

the capacity to do the job you require of it.

Never mix chemicals together unless recommended to do so in the maker's instructions. Several fungicides and insecticides are compatible and may safely be mixed and applied together, which is a great saving of time and energy. For this information, check the label for instructions.

A range of chemicals to cover most garden requirements is given on page 124.

THE GREENHOUSE OR CONSERVATORY

A greenhouse, which may possibly double as a conservatory or sun lounge, gives a lot more scope to and increases the fun of gardening. Greenhouse gardening calls for additional skills and offers hours of pleasure in experimenting and growing a range of more unusual plants. It is somewhere to enjoy the garden on wet, windy and cold days, and makes it possible to establish flowers and vegetables before planting out in the garden. A greenhouse also helps to provide flowering plants for decoration in the house during the winter and early spring months.

If possible, the greenhouse should be sited so that it takes maximum advantage of all the light and sunshine available. It is also a bonus if it can be close to the house so that water and electricity supplies can be easily laid on although neither of these is essential.

Whether to heat the greenhouse or not depends on what you can afford, but if it is at all possible, I do recommend supplying sufficient heat to be able to keep the temperature in winter to a minimum of 7°C(45°F) allowing a much wider choice of plants which can be grown. This is the level of heat at which I maintain my own greenhouse, and the information given each month relates to a greenhouse in which this amount of heat is available. The scope of such a greenhouse can be greatly increased if an electric propagating frame is installed, so that it is possible to achieve higher temperatures for seed raising and rooting cuttings.

Composts All the operations such as seed sowing and potting require the use of special sterilised and prepared composts. Of these there are two main kinds: the John Innes seed and potting composts and the peat-based composts. Except for a plant which will be left a long time in one container, and for which the soil-based John Innes composts are preferable, it doesn't matter which is used. The John Innes potting composts are obtainable in three grades: 1, 2 or 3. The number indicates different quantities of fertiliser, No. 1 having the least and No. 3 the most.

Garden Frame This is a very useful accessory to the greenhouse, forming as it does a sort of halfway stage between greenhouse and garden. It enables many plants raised in the greenhouse to be acclimatised gradually to outdoor conditions, as well as providing additional sheltered growing space. As with greenhouses, a heated frame offers more scope than an unheated one, and this can be done fairly easily with soil-warming cables and air-warming cables around the sides. Unheated frames are used for hardening off bedding plants, for rooting cuttings, as a standing place for plants such as carnations and cyclamen in summer, for the growing of cucumbers in summer and lettuce in winter, and for starting off the bowls and pots of bulbs intended for indoors.

IN CONCLUSION

In this book I have tried to give a working programme which takes into account all the most important aspects of gardening, whilst bearing in mind that the majority of gardeners are limited with regard to the amount of time available for gardening. The fascination of gardening is that there are no hard and fast rules, I have my own ways of doing things and find them successful, other people differ in their views and are equally successful.

A sense of achievement and the enjoyment which comes from the pursuit are all that is important.

January

'If the grass grows
in Janiveer
It grows the worse
for it all the year'

January is likely to be an uncertain month with regard to
the weather and what we do in the garden depends on what's
happening out of doors. But if it's snowing take heart because snow
does the ground good and many plants will be all the better for it.

It is important to take every opportunity to try to complete
jobs begun earlier in the winter such as fruit tree pruning
and spraying and any digging. But if the soil is in an unworkable
condition, and this is if it sticks to your boots or the spade, then
keep off it. Finish any construction work you may have on hand
and when you are finally defeated by the weather remember
that forward planning makes gardening easier and gives better
results. Much of your time during the early part of the month can
be spent in the comfort of the fireside turning over the pages
of seed catalogues to see what you intend to order
for the coming year.

When selecting flowers the choice of colours should be made
carefully and planting schemes worked out to take into account
the heights of those chosen. Even more important in many ways
is the planning of the vegetable garden: decide first what
vegetables you want to grow and then choose varieties which
will give you a continuity of cropping. A suggested list of
vegetables is given on page 117.

There is little doubt that the introduction of the F_1 hybrid
varieties (resulting from a cross between species or
varieties) has brought about improvements in many plants.
However, the seed is expensive so we cannot afford to have many
failures. Far too many seeds are either wasted through buying
more than are actually needed, or they are lost through sowing
too early, or not providing a sufficiently high temperature,
or giving too little or too much water. When the seeds arrive,
put them in air-tight containers and keep them in a cool place
until sowing time.

CHECK LIST
Plant deciduous shrubs
Prune ornamental trees
Rake lawn
Lime vegetable plot
Chit seed potatoes
Finish spraying fruit
Box up dahlia tubers
Repot fuchsias

Outside

TREES AND SHRUBS
Planting I like to see the majority of deciduous trees, shrubs and roses planted before Christmas if this is possible. Planting can continue this month whenever the soil is workable. Old potting compost, peat or composted tree bark will help if mixed with the soil. All these are good rooting media which will enable the plant to form new roots much more quickly.

You may have been given shrubs or roses for Christmas, and if the soil is unfit for planting these should be kept either in a shed with the roots moist or heeled in the garden with the roots covered with soil. Losses and failures can often be traced to allowing the roots to dry out before planting.

Check all trees, shrubs and roses planted last autumn and refirm them if they have been lifted by wind or frost.

Heeling in. Lay shrubs in a trench.

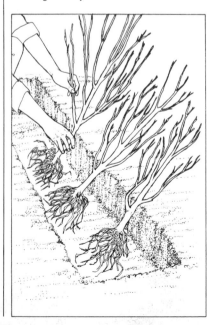

Pruning Look over ornamental trees and shrubs and remove any dead or diseased wood. Any suckers growing from the base of trees should be cut back to the point from which they originate. This may be from the root or from the base of the stems.

Any large cuts should be painted over with a sealing compound or a wax to prevent entry of disease. Keep pruning to a minimum as you may be cutting away branches which would have provided flowers later on if left.

General care Shake snow from evergreen shrubs to prevent the branches breaking

FLOWERS
Towards the end of the month protect buds of the hardy primulas and crocuses from the birds by stranding black cotton backwards and forwards over them. The cotton should be

Return the soil and firm in.

supported on sticks 15 to 20 cm (6 to 8 in) above the plants.
The rock garden Check to see if any plants have been lifted by frosts and firm in if necessary.

THE LAWN
This may well be looking a little tired but because of the likelihood of wet conditions it is not generally speaking, advisable to do much work on it. If the weather is reasonable then rake it over with a springbok rake to scatter worm casts and clear away any debris.

Preparations can be made for laying turf next month: break up the soil with a fork to a depth of 13 to 15 cm (5 to 6 in), make it firm by treading over the surface and rake the surface down finely.

VEGETABLES
In the vegetable garden the important job is liming. I make a point of liming one-third of the garden each year, applying hydrated lime at the rate of 110 to 170 g to sq m (4 to 6 oz to sq yd). Don't lime ground where you intend to plant potatoes: limed areas are used mainly for cabbages and other members of the brassica family and also peas and beans. Basic slag is a good source of lime for a heavy soil as it helps to improve texture; this should be applied early to allow time for it to be broken down into a soluble form. Apply at the rate of 170 to 225 g to sq m (6 to 8 oz to sq yd). In addition to containing lime, basic slag provides phosphate—an essential food.

Any winter digging should be completed and the soil left

in large lumps. Dig in manure, garden compost or other humus-forming substances (page 13), but do not do this if the ground is intended for root crops as it will cause malformation of the roots.

When growing vegetables it is essential to plan ahead so that you know what crop is going where. In this way, the correct fertiliser regime can be used. **Crops in the garden this month** Brussels sprouts, winter cabbage, parsnips, Jerusalem artichokes, leeks and, in the milder parts of the country, winter cauliflower. This last should have a leaf or two broken over the curds to give frost protection.

When lifting Jerusalem artichokes select the smaller tubers to put aside for planting in February or early March.

It is a good idea to lift extra parsnips and cover these with sand in a sheltered part of the garden so that they will be accessible in the event of severe weather.

Early rhubarb Cover a couple of roots with straw, put unturned tubs over them and pile more straw over the tubs for extra protection and to encourage early shoots.

FRUIT

Ideally all pruning of fruit trees should be finished before Christmas, but if not it should be done as early in January as possible.

Apples, pears, plums and cherries will all benefit from a spray with tar oil winter wash to kill off the overwintering eggs of many of the pests. This must be applied according to maker's instructions, and if fruit trees are growing among vegetables then any crops must be protected from spray because it will scorch and spoil them.

It is still possible to plant all kinds of fruit trees.

Crop rotation

When growing vegetables, it is advisable to change the position of the individual crops each year in order to prevent the build up of pests and diseases. Moving the crops also allows for the fact that different vegetables take different amounts of nutrients from the soil and so require different amounts or types of fertiliser or manure.

The area available is divided into three plots and used as shown in the diagram—the crops, with their appropriate fertiliser requirements, being moved on a three-year rotation. Permanent crops such as rhubarb and herbs should be left undisturbed.

YEAR 1

PLOT A
ROOT CROPS
Apply general fertiliser before sowing

PLOT B
BRASSICAS
Apply lime if necessary and general fertiliser before sowing

PLOT C
LEGUMES, LEEKS, LEAFY CROPS
Dig in compost or manure

YEAR 2

PLOT A
LEGUMES

PLOT B
ROOT CROPS

PLOT C
BRASSICAS

YEAR 3

PLOT A
BRASSICAS

PLOT B
LEGUMES

PLOT C
ROOT CROPS

Check the grease bands put on the trees in the autumn (page 89) and if necessary renew the grease.

Examine trees for canker wounds and if there are any cut away the affected bark and wood until clean tissue is reached. Paint over the areas with bituminous paint or a sealing compound.

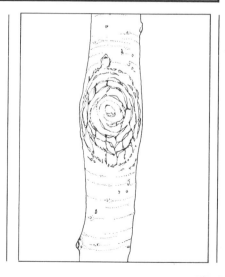

Canker shows up as areas of split, peeling and gnarled bark which may spread to encircle the stem.

January

Plants of the Month

The garden may well be looking rather bare this month, although there is the hope of seeing the first bulbs—the snowdrops, crocus and iris—unless the weather is very cold and snowy.
As with the other winter months, we must rely on the conifers, evergreens and some of the good winter-flowering shrubs, such as the jasmine and mahonias, to give the interest which, hopefully, will entice us out into the garden again.

SHRUBS

Chimonanthus (Winter Sweet).   Very aptly named, *Chimonanthus fragrans* produces yellow, fragrant flowers in winter but plants take several years to begin flowering. Growing to a height of 1·5 to 2·5 m (5 to 8 ft), this is a shrub for a sunny, very sheltered position, preferably by a wall, and in good soil. No regular pruning required, but some of the older branches can be cut out after flowering if desired.

Cornus (Dogwood)   Several kinds of dogwood are especially valuable for their colourful young stems in winter, these include the red-stemmed *Cornus alba* Sibirica and the yellow-stemmed *C. stolonifera* Flaviramea. They make shrubs 2 to 2·5 m (6 to 8 ft) tall, and should be hard pruned in spring to encourage a good supply of young growth. They will succeed in an open or shady position but prefer a moist soil, although this is not necessary.

Garrya (Silk Tassel Bush)   This evergreen shrub is useful for a sheltered sunny wall or other very sheltered position, and ordinary well-drained soil. It carries impressive, long silvery catkins in January and February and will grow to 3·5 m (12 ft) tall. There are male and female plants and the catkins are longer on the former. No pruning required but overcrowded shoots can be removed in spring.

Lonicera (Honeysuckle)   There are two shrubby semi-evergreen honeysuckles which produce small fragrant creamy white flowers in winter. *Lonicera fragrantissima* and *L. standishii* grow to 1·5 to 2 m (5 to 6 ft) in height in any reasonably good soil, in sun or partial shade.

Salix (Willow)   Another plant which is grown for its lovely red shoots in winter is *Salix alba* Britzensis and there is also a yellow-stemmed form *S.a.* Vitellina. Both should be hard pruned in March to ensure plenty of new growth. Plant

1 The silk tassel bush, *Garrya elliptica*
2 *Viburnum bodnantense*
3 Snowdrops, *Galanthus nivalis*
4 *Iris reticulata* hybrid 5 Cineraria

them in a sunny or lightly shaded position and ordinary or moist soil.

Viburnum   Evergreen winter-flowering kinds include *Viburnum burkwoodii* and *V. tinus* (Laurustinus). Both have white flowers which will last into spring. *Tinus* grows to 3 m (10 ft) or so, *burkwoodii* is smaller to 2.5 m (8 ft.).

This useful group of shrubs also provides some deciduous kinds which flower now. *V. bodnantense* grows to 3 m (10 ft), *fragrans* to 2·5 m (8 ft), and both have pink flowers.

All the viburnums require a sunny or lightly shaded position and reasonably fertile soil. If necessary, prune after flowering, removing some of the older and overcrowded stems.

FLOWERING PLANTS

Pulmonaria (Lungwort)   A hardy border plant suitable for any ordinary soil and lightly shaded position. The foliage is often spotted with white, the flowers are pink shading to blue or violet. Most grow to about 25 cm (10 in) tall. To increase, divide in spring or autumn.

BULBS

Crocus   Some of the earliest kinds will now be in flower, especially the species such as *aureus*, *imperati* and *tomasinianus*. Plant them on the margins of beds or borders, or in lawns, placing the corms between 5 and 8 cm (2 and 3 in) deep. Leave undisturbed after flowering.

Eranthis (Winter Aconites)   With their glowing yellow flowers these can be relied upon to provide a touch of colour between now and March. Suited to a shady border under deciduous trees and shrubs or on rock gardens. Plant 5 cm (2 in) deep and the same distance apart. Leave undisturbed after flowering. *E.* Tubergenii is a particularly handsome kind.

Galanthus (Snowdrop)   These eagerly awaited flowers are suited to any soil and an open or shaded position, either in the garden or on the rock garden. Plant 5 cm (2 in) deep and 2.5 cm (1 in) apart. *G. nivalis* is the usual kind together with its varieties S. Arnott and Atkinsii. Can be lifted and divided after flowering if necessary.

Iris   *Iris histrio* blue and yellow; *histrioides* blue, white and yellow, and *reticulata* and its varieties, violet, purple or yellow are the kinds to grow for flowering now. All grow to between 10 and 12 cm (4 and 8 in) high and are ideal for the rock garden or the edge of a border. Leave undisturbed after

flowering. They can also be planted in pots in the autumn for flowering indoors.

VEGETABLES IN THE GARDEN

Jerusalem artichokes, sprouting broccoli, Brussels sprouts, cauliflower, celery, leeks, parsnips, savoy and other winter cabbage, spinach and turnips.

INSIDE

Azalea   The Indian azaleas are marvellous pot plants for a January to April display, with flowers in a wide range of shades of pink, red and white. Remove flowers as they fade and repot after flowering. Keep pots out of doors during the frost-free months. Water and feed regularly.

Cineraria   There is a large range of varieties of this wonderful greenhouse plant, with flowers in blue, purple, crimson and scarlet, often with a white central disc. Take great care when watering.

January

Inside

A greenhouse was once considered a luxury, but today it is looked on as more of a necessity. It's a place where we can grow early seedlings, where we can work when the outside weather is inclement and it will provide flowering plants throughout most of the year.

With the rise in the cost of all forms of heating, many greenhouses are now without heat, but there are some plants which will flower in an unheated greenhouse in winter. These include bulbs, primroses, the Pacific strain of polyanthus, camellias and other hardy plants and shrubs, such as ribes and forsythia, which can be grown in pots to give a fine display.

If the greenhouse is unheated then a propagating frame is essential for raising seedlings and cuttings early in the year.

Seed sowing can begin this month in a heated propagating frame.

In this way the heating is confined to a small area and is less costly.

It is unwise to sow any seeds at the moment unless a temperature of at least 13 to 16°C (55 to 60°F) can be maintained.

Washing down the greenhouse This is a task which can be done when the weather outside is bad. Wash the glass inside and out, scrub the paintwork, clean the propagating frame as well as pots, seed trays and boxes in readiness for seed sowing.

Care with watering Take the utmost care with watering all pot plants until the days lengthen and the weather improves. Always err on the dry side; this does not mean giving dribbles of water, but leaving the plants until the compost is dry, then giving them a thorough soaking and no more until the compost is dry again. Water early in the day otherwise you will leave plants

wet throughout the night.

General care Any dead or yellowing leaves from geraniums (zonal pelargoniums), regal pelargoniums, fuchsias and other plants should be picked off. These can be the beginning of botrytis which can cause serious losses in the greenhouse with the lower temperatures.

Geraniums lifted from the garden in late September and early October will need care to get them through the winter. Keep them reasonably dry and in the lightest position.

Seed sowing Sweet peas can be sown in pots or boxes. I prefer to use the small peat pots so that seedlings can be planted with little or no root disturbance.

In order to grow really large onions I like to make a start now sowing Mammoth and Kelsae in peat pots for planting out in April.

Bulbs Bring more bulbs in pots and bowls inside. Keep them in cool conditions to begin with until the buds show.

Tubers and corms Dahlia tubers required for cuttings should be cleaned up and the stems cut back to within an inch or two of the roots. Put the tubers into boxes and cover with a mixture of equal parts soil, peat and sand. Keep reasonably dry until the middle of this month, then, given water, they will begin to produce their young shoots which will make the cuttings.

Inspect the tubers of begonias and gloxinias for signs of disease. These need a minimum temperature of 7°C (45°F) if they are to survive the winter so it may be necessary

to keep them in a spare room in the house.

Carnations Continue to take cuttings of perpetual-flowering carnations and root them in pure sand in a propagating frame. Pot on into 3-in pots any cuttings that have rooted.

Chrysanthemums Continue to cut plants down as they finish flowering. Those chosen as stock plants should be shaken from the compost and put into boxes, each one labelled, with new compost. For this a mixture of equal parts of peat and sand will be sufficient. These must be kept in a light position to ensure the growth of sturdy shoots which will be used to make cuttings.

Fuchsias The compost in the pots has been kept reasonably dry since late November so the plants are completely dormant. Cut back all side branches (the ones which produced flowers last year) to within one or two buds. Then, shake the compost from the roots and repot each plant into the smallest pot into which it is possible to get the roots. By potting into smaller pots now,

Boxing up dahlia tubers to start them into growth.

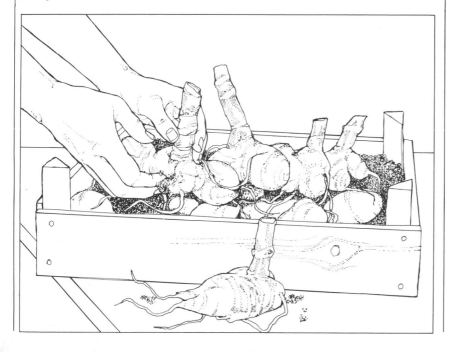

it will allow for potting into larger pots later, when the roots need fresh compost and more space. For this potting use John Innes potting compost No. 1 or a peat-based compost and shake it down between the roots before attempting to firm. Give each one a thorough watering and then no more until the compost is really dry again.

Forced rhubarb The first sticks should be ready for pulling this month.

Potatoes I think that in an average garden it is only advisable to grow early varieties of potato; maincrop potatoes can usually be purchased at a reasonable price and the ground can be put to better use.

Seed potatoes are available in January and these should be chitted in readiness for planting out in March. To do this, set them in trays in single layers with the eye ends uppermost and keep in a light position in a frost-free place. This will encourage the production of sturdy young shoots. Popular early varieties are the Arran Pilot, Homeguard, Ulster Chieftain and (my favourite) Foremost.

Chitting potatoes *Above* The seed potatoes arranged in boxes and, *below*, a well-sprouted example.

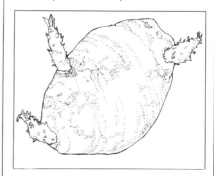

HOUSE PLANTS

Many of those flowering plants that were in the house over Christmas may be getting a little tired in the warm, dry atmosphere of the house. It is marvellous how these plants, including the ever-popular cyclamen, *Primula obconica*, poinsettias and azaleas, will improve with a week or two in the greenhouse under slightly cooler conditions and in better light. It is, I consider, the lack of light which does more harm to these plants than anything else.

Foliage plants, such as the rubber tree, monstera and others with large glossy leaves, will look brighter and be all the better for a light sponging to remove any dust. There are various leaf shines which can be used, or a teaspoonful of milk in a cup of lukewarm water does the job. Wipe the leaves with a soft cloth or sponge, otherwise they may be marked and damaged.

25

CHECK LIST

Prune summer-flowering
  shrubs
Make lawn from turf
Divide hardy border plants
Feed fruit trees
Prune gooseberries and
  raspberries
Feed cauliflower and greens
Prepare cuttings of geraniums,
  chrysanthemums and fuchsias
First sowings under glass

February

'February fill
the dyke
with what thou
does like'

February is often remarkable for being an excessively wet
or snowy month during which it may be impossible to do much
around the garden. There is, however, plenty of work to be done
in the greenhouse although unless this is kept heated it is
still too early for sowing the majority of seeds. I have found
that lining the greenhouse with polythene has a marked effect
on preventing heat loss as it is possible to maintain temperatures
up to about 5°C (10°F) higher with the same amount of heat.
When doing this, make sure you do not cover the ventilators
as, even in winter, circulation of air is an important factor
in preventing a stagnant atmosphere and onset of disease.

If soil conditions are good, free from frost and not too wet,
I suggest you make the most of every opportunity to continue
planting trees, shrubs, roses and other plants. It is also a good idea
to check those planted earlier and refirm the soil if necessary.

Severe gales at this time of year may play havoc in many
gardens causing damage to both trees and shrubs. Where conifers
have been blown about the branches can be tied back to keep
the neat shape of the trees, provided they are not broken.
Any broken branches must be cut back. In most cases, these trees
will gradually reshape themselves. Where large branches have to be
cut off, paint over the cut surface with either a wax preparation
or bituminous paint.

While the birds can do untold damage to fruit trees and bushes,
they can also do damage to flowering trees and shrubs—bullfinches
are largely responsible for this. In the case of large shrubs
it is difficult to protect them with netting. There are various
bird repellents in spray form which make the buds distasteful
to the birds, however, if we get heavy rain, spraying must be
repeated or time and money will have been wasted.

Outside

TREES AND SHRUBS

Pruning In many parts of the country rose pruning can begin now. There are those who prune before Christmas but I prefer to leave mine until March (see page 37 for details).

Large-flowered hybrid clematis growing on west-facing walls may sometimes start into early growth and it may be better to prune these now rather than leaving them to March. Cut the stems back to within 60 to 75 cm (2 to 2½ ft) of the ground to a good well developed bud. Such hard pruning encourages strong growth and good flowers. *Clematis montana* and its varieties should not be pruned now but left until after flowering.

Summer-flowering shrubs such as *Buddleia davidii*, caryopteris, *Hydrangea paniculata*, deciduous ceanothus, potentillas and hardy fuchsias can also be pruned now. In every case the shoots made last year are cut back hard to within an inch or two of the old wood. These are all shrubs which flower on young wood which will develop over the next few months.

Prune the winter-flowering shrubs such as *Jasminum nudiflorum* as soon as flowering has finished. Cut out some of the old wood, prune back thinner branches and train in the young green branches which will produce new shoots and flowers.

After pruning, feed with a general fertiliser and mulch with garden compost, peat, or composted tree bark.

FLOWERS

Planting Now is the time when those hardy border plants which have not been disturbed for three years can be lifted and divided. I like to lift and label the roots and cover them with polythene to protect them from drying out and then prepare the ground, digging in manure, garden compost or peat and adding a dressing of general fertiliser or bonemeal. The root clumps are prised apart by using two forks back to back, and small pieces from the outside with 3, 4, 5 or 6 young shoots, are used for replanting. Discard the hard pieces from the centre.

Those plants most likely to need this treatment are monarda, lupins, Michaelmas daisies, heleniums, rudbeckias, delphiniums, *Sedum spectabile* and *Sedum* Autumn Joy, lysimachia, border phlox, achillea, echinops, erigerons and *Chrysanthemum maximum*, shasta daisies.

Those hardy plants which are not to be lifted will benefit from feeding. Use a general garden fertiliser, applied according to maker's instructions, and stir it lightly into the soil.

Lily of the valley crowns can be planted now, set them with their points just below the surface of the soil and 5 to 8 cm (2 to 3 in) apart.

The rock garden Topdress with a mixture of peat, soil, and sand in equal parts to which a little bonemeal has been added.

THE LAWN

The grass should now be beginning to grow and if there is a lot of moss present then the whole lawn can be treated with a mosskiller applied according to maker's instructions.

Light raking will help to comb out any dead grass and, if a mosskiller is not used, then topdress with a mixture of fine soil, peat and sand to which a lawn fertiliser has been added.

It is essential to complete any turfing this month and also to prepare the ground for sowing grass seed later.

Make good any bare patches by cutting squares of healthy turf, laying these over the patches and marking round the turves with an edging iron or spade. Remove the marked sections and put the good turves in their place, leaving them a little proud of the surrounding turf to allow for settling.

VEGETABLES

About the middle of the month put cloches in position where the first seeds will be sown in March. This will allow the soil to dry and warm up that much faster and can make a difference of as much as three weeks in the gathering of the first crops.

It is possible to sow the broad bean variety Aquadulce now in many parts of the country. Sow 5 cm (2 in) deep and 5 cm (6 in) apart in double rows 23 cm (9 in) apart with 1 m (3 ft) between each pair or rows.

Plant rhubarb and also herbs—chives, thyme, sage and mint—dividing plants if necessary.

If sage has been damaged by frost, it can be cut back to 23 cm (9 in) or so and new shoots will grow from the base.

Plant Jerusalem artichokes towards the end of the month, setting these 13 cm (5 in) deep, 38 cm (15 in) apart and leaving 75 cm (2½ ft) between rows.

Feeding Spring cabbage, sprouting broccoli and late winter cauliflower should be fed with a general fertiliser sprinkled along the rows at a rate of 55 g per m row (2 oz per yd row).

Onions Transplant autumn-sown onions, spacing them 23 cm (9 in) apart in rows 38 cm (15 in) apart.

FRUIT

Feeding This is the time for feeding fruit. I use a rose fertiliser because it has extra potash and added magnesium and sprinkle a dessertspoonful around each strawberry plant, keeping it away from the centre and lightly scratching it into the soil with a fork.

Feed other fruit at the following rates: a handful to each yard of raspberry row, 110 g (4 oz) round each black-currant, 85 to 110 g (3 to 4 oz) round each gooseberry, 170 to 225 g (6 to 8 oz) round each apple tree and all trained trees and cordons.

Planting and pruning Continue planting all kinds of fruit.

Raspberries which were planted in the autumn should be cut back to a bud 20 or 23 cm (8 or 9 in) from the ground, and autumn-planted blackcurrants should be cut back to 15 or 20 cm (6 or 8 in).

Established raspberry plants should have new shoots tied in securely, and the tops of the canes pruned back to within an inch or two of the top wire.

I usually prune gooseberries this month, having left them unpruned because the birds tend to take the buds during the winter. Doing this means that the birds take the buds

Making a lawn from turf

Always buy the best quality turves available, avoiding those which contain a lot of weeds and poor quality grasses.

Lay the turf on a dry day but when the soil is moist and check that the soil surface is as level as possible and raked finely— hollows below the turves (see inset drawing) result in an uneven surface which wears badly.

It is important to make sure that the turves are bonded like bricks and that each one fits closely to the adjacent ones and is in good contact with the soil. As the turves are put in position, beat them lightly with a spade. Finish by sprinkling a dressing of peat and soil along the crevices.

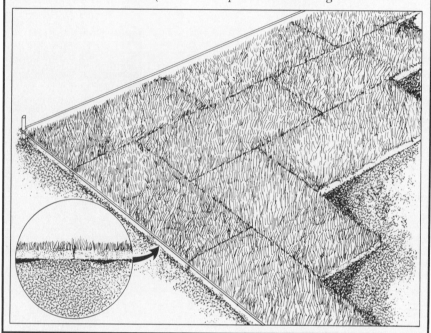

which will be pruned off rather than those on the older wood which will form the fruit. When pruning, cut off any dead, diseased and crossing branches and remove the tips of remaining branches. All lateral growths are cut back to about 5 cm (2 in).

Protect the bushes from birds by draping net over them and supporting this on a framework of poles or canes. A jam jar placed on the top of each cane will keep the net in position.

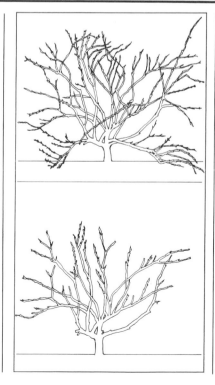

When pruning gooseberries, keep the centre of the bush open, remove diseased wood and low branches, cut the tips from the main shoots and reduce all side shoots to 5 cm (2 in).

February

Plants of the Month

This month we are still relying on the shrubs that were in flower in January to give us some colour, although many more of the early bulbs should be coming into flower. The heathers, *Erica carnea* and *E. darleyensis* (page 114) and their many varieties are also wonderful for providing winter colour, but much depends on how severe the winter is, and February often has the worst weather of the season.

SHRUBS

Cornus mas (Cornelian Cherry)   This deciduous shrub has small clusters of yellow flowers produced on the bare branches in February and March. It is easily grown in any soil and position, and reaches a height of about 4·5 m (15 ft). The flowers are followed by edible, red fruits.

Corylopsis   A deciduous shrub for deep moist soil and a sheltered position away from the morning sun, *Corylopsis spicata* has scented primrose-yellow flowers that appear before the leaves, and grows to about 2 m (6 ft) high. *C. pauciflora* is similar but smaller, to only 1 m (3 ft) or so. No pruning required.

Corylus (Hazel)   Two decorative forms of the familiar catkin-bearing deciduous common hazel are Aurea with golden leaves, and Contorta with twisted branches. Both require a good soil and sunny open position, and will grow to between 3 to 4·5 m (10 to 15 ft). No pruning required.

Daphne mezereum (The Mezereon)   Fragrant, pink, rose-purple or white-flowered deciduous shrub growing to 1·25 m (4 ft). It needs a cool, moist but free draining soil, and will grow on chalk. No pruning required.

Elaeagnus   The yellow-splashed leaves of the evergreen *Elaeagnus pungens maculata* are a cheerful sight throughout the winter, and will be especially welcome this month when they will reflect every glimpse of sunshine. It grows to about 1·5 m (5 ft) and has no particular requirements with regard to soil or position.

Hamamelis (Witch Hazel)   Deciduous shrub growing up to about 3·5 m (12 ft) high, which prefers a good rich soil and sunny or lightly shaded position. The flowers are yellow and scented, and some species, such as *Hamamelis mollis*, have autumn-tinted foliage. No pruning needed.

FLOWERING PLANTS

Bergenia (Megasea, Elephant's Ears)   This hardy border plant has large leathery evergreen foliage and, in early spring, heavy heads of white, pink or reddish-purple flowers. Grows to about 38 cm (15 in) in any ordinary soil and sunny or lightly shaded position. Divide in spring or autumn.

Viola (Sweet Violet)   There are numerous varieties of this delightful small herbaceous plant (*Viola odorata*), with white, pink, mauve, lavender and purple-blue flowers, some double or semi-double. They require a cool shady position and ordinary soil, with some peat or leaf mould added.

BULBS

Chionodoxa (Glory of the Snow)   Blue or white flowering bulbs growing to 20 cm (8 in) high, best suited to a well drained sunny border or rock garden. Plant 2.5 cm (1 in) apart and 8 cm (3 in) deep in autumn. Lift and replant every three years or so.

Crocus More varieties should now be coming into flower. The birds enjoy eating the petals, and may strip the flowers completely unless they are protected in some way, such as by stranding black cotton over them. Leave corms undisturbed after flowering.

Erythronium (Dog's Tooth Violet) Growing to 15 cm (6 in) with pink flowers, *Erythronium dens canis* is an unusual plant for a sheltered moist and lightly shaded position. Plant 8 cm (3 in) deep and 5 cm (2 in) apart in early autumn and leave undisturbed.

VEGETABLES IN THE GARDEN

Jerusalem artichoke, sprouting broccoli, Brussels sprouts, late cauliflowers, leeks, parsnips, Savoy cabbage, lettuce and spring onions.

INSIDE

Camellia japonica The numerous varieties of this evergreen shrub are excellent, both for the cool greenhouse and a very sheltered position out of doors. Flower colours are in all shades from white through pink to red and may be single, semi-double and double. Mostly up to 3 m (8 ft) tall, but may grow to 6 m (20 ft) in the right position outside. They need a lime-free soil and are happiest in partial shade. No pruning required; overgrown bushes can be cut back in spring with a loss of bloom in the following year.

Primula The many coloured varieties of *P. kewensis*, *malacoides*, *obconica* and *sinensis* sown in the summer of the previous year should still be providing much of the flower in the cool greenhouse.

Other plants in flower indoors include azaleas, cyclamen, cinerarias and the remaining bulbs in bowls.

February

Inside

Increase ventilation on sunny days and continue to water with care.

Seed sowing   If there is a warm propagating frame in the greenhouse where a minimum temperature of 15°C (59°F) can be maintained the following seeds can be sown: gloxinias, large flowered begonias, *Begonia semperflorens*, streptocarpus, and, towards the end of the month, tomatoes for planting in a fairly warm house in March.

If a minimum temperature of 7°C (45°F) can be maintained then the following vegetables can be sown: broad beans, lettuce (Little Gem) summer cauliflower (All Year Round or Snowball), summer cabbage (Hispi, Primo), Brussels sprouts and leeks. I also like to make a sowing of peas, such as Feltham First, planting 3 or 4 peas in each 3½-in pot.

Keep all the vegetable seedlings as near to the glass as possible to keep plants growing sturdily. Some of them will be used for planting out under cloches in March or early April.

Sweet peas sown last month should be ready for stopping. Remove the tips from the first shoots to encourage strong young shoots from the base. If sowing has not been done, then there is still time to do so.

Begonias and gloxinias   Some of the tubers may be showing signs of producing new shoots and these can be started in seed trays. Place the tubers 8 cm (3 in) apart on a layer of moist peat.

Carnations   Continue to take cuttings and to pot on into 3-in pots those which have rooted.

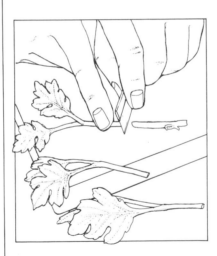

Taking chrysanthemum cuttings
Remove the shoot and trim the end; then insert in pots or boxes.

Chrysanthemums   If a heated propagator is available, then cuttings of the indoor flowering chrysanthemums can be taken. The roots which were boxed up last month should now be producing good shoots 8 to 10 cm (3 to 4 in) long. Cut the shoot straight across with a sharp knife immediately below a leaf joint and treat each cutting with hormone rooting powder. Insert the cuttings in pots filled with a mixture of peat and sand in equal parts.

After watering, place the pots in the propagating frame and shade with newspaper on sunny days. The cuttings should be rooted in about three weeks.

Roots of outdoor-flowering chrysanthemums must now be brought into the greenhouse to encourage shoots to grow.

Geraniums   Plants which have been overwintered can be cut back to within 20 or 23 cm (8 or 9 in) of the roots. All the old soil should be shaken from the roots and they can then be repotted into small pots. Give one watering and let them get really dry before giving them any more.

The tips which have been cut off can be used to make cuttings. If inserted in a mixture of peat and sand, kept in a temperature of 7 to 10°C (45 to 50°F) and watered sparingly they will form good plants for planting out later in spring.

Geranium and fuchsia cuttings taken in autumn can be potted now. Use John Innes potting compost No. 1 or a peat-based compost and, if the compost is moist, leave them for a few days before giving any

water. Spread some sheets of newspaper over the cuttings at night to protect them from frost.
Fuchsias The old fuchsia plants which were pruned back last month may now be producing young shoots. As these develop, gradually increase the amount of water given to the plants.

Cuttings made from these young shoots will make good plants for setting out at the end of May. Dip the ends in rooting powder and insert them in sandy soil around the edge of a 3-in pot. Keep in the propagating frame until rooted.
Schizanthus Pot on these and other spring flowering annuals into 6- or 8-in pots.

HOUSE PLANTS

Now is a good time to take cuttings from plants such as ivy, philodendron (sweetheart vine), *Cissus antarctica* (kangaroo vine) and *Rhoicissus rhomboidea* (grape ivy). Cut pieces of shoot with at least two leaves on each, cutting just below the lower leaf and just above the top one. Remove the lower leaf, dip the cut end in rooting powder and put it in a mixture of peat and sand. Place in a propagating frame or cover with a polythene bag and keep in a fairly warm situation.

Seed Sowing

Equipment needed for seed sowing includes clean seed trays or pots, a proprietary brand of seed sowing compost and a piece of wood to smooth the surface of the compost. The method is as follows: fill a clean seed tray with a ready mixed seed sowing compost. Firm the compost with the fingers and press down with a piece of wood or the bottom of a pot to get a flat level surface. The compost must then be thoroughly moistened, either by standing the box in a shallow container of water and leaving it until the moisture shows on the surface or by using a watering can fitted with a fine rose.

Sow the seeds thinly by sprinkling them from the packet or by pouring them into one hand and using the finger and thumb of the other hand to distribute them as evenly as possible. Cover the seeds with a sprinkling of soil, and place a sheet of glass and piece of paper over the top. Leave in a fairly warm place until the seeds have germinated and then remove the glass and paper. The seedlings will need to be pricked out as soon as they are large enough to handle.

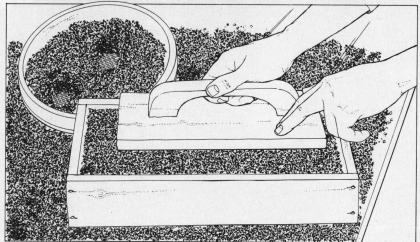

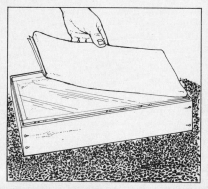

March

'If March comes in like a lion
it goes out like a lamb'

March is the month when we welcome the most fascinating
season of the year—spring. It is a month notable for its winds
and I like to see the dust blowing from the garden path. I can
remember my father saying that March dust was worth
a pound a peck, by which he meant that once you see dust
blowing off the path you know the surface of the soil is beginning
to dry, and this will allow the making of a seed bed.

This is a busy month when seed sowing and planting can begin
in the vegetable and flower garden, but you have got to be guided
by the weather and condition of the soil. It is a waste of seeds
to sow them before the soil has warmed up sufficiently
and the best barometers I know are the hedges—when these
start showing green it's an indication that the soil temperature
is rising and we can begin the sowing and planting.

March sees the end of the season for planting deciduous
trees, shrubs and roses which have either been brought in,
or moved from one part of the garden to another. The earlier
the planting can be done the better as they need time
to get established before any dry weather sets in. Many
shrubs are planted too deeply in the soil. Both azaleas
and rhododendrons are shallow-rooted plants and must have their
roots near the surface. Also, they like plenty of peat mixed
into the soil as planting is done. Other trees and shrubs
may take much longer to get away, or give up the ghost
entirely if they are planted too deeply.

March

Outside

TREES AND SHRUBS

Pruning   Pruning of the large-flowered clematis, late-summer flowering and also the winter-flowering shrubs can continue this month, and after pruning all the shrubs will benefit from a dressing of general fertiliser and a mulch of garden compost, peat or composted bark.

Spraying and feeding roses Once the rose pruning is finished, it is important to spray with a fungicide to prevent any over-wintering spores on the branches and on the soil from springing into growth. When spraying, use a fine forceful spray to make sure that all the branches and the soil surface are completely covered with the fungicide. Fork the soil over lightly before spraying.

Next comes feeding, and for this I use a rose fertiliser and sprinkle 55 g (2 oz) around each bush, keeping it away from the stem. The larger climbing roses will get 55 to 110 g (2 to 4 oz) around each one and the same will apply to the shrub and species roses. Towards the end of the month apply a mulch around the roots using garden compost, peat or composted tree bark.

FLOWERS

Hardy border plants   By March I like to be well ahead with the lifting, dividing and replanting of the hardy perennials. However, when February lives up to its reputation and is wet or snowy, this is a job which may continue through March to early April if necessary.

The rock garden   Remove any protection from the plants.

Preparation for sowing annuals   If it is intended to sow hardy annuals at the end of this month or early April, then it is essential to prepare the soil early to allow a short space of time for natural settling. These flowers need an open sunny position and a soil which is not too rich. Therefore, it will not be wise to dig in manure, too much garden compost, or apply too much concentrated fertiliser. I have always found a sprinkling of sulphate of potash not more than 25 g to the sq m (1 oz to the sq yd), does much to provide an abundance of flower with good colour and good scent on most of the annuals.

Pansies or violas can be sown out of doors in a nursery bed.

Bulbs   Those which have finished flowering indoors can be tipped out of their pots or bowls and replanted in the garden to finish their growth.

THE LAWN

If the lawn wasn't treated with mosskiller last month, then it should be done now. Feeding is advisable to help the grass recover from the winter and thicken up to form a rich green covering. For this feeding I advise you to use an all-seasons lawn food. It is early as yet to use a lawn fertiliser with an added selective weed-killer.

The first cut   It is often possible to do the first mowing sometime during March. It is important not to let the grass get too long before its first cut, otherwise the blades of grass near the ground become yellow and the lawn looks very patchy after mowing. For this cut the bottom blade of the mower should be set to cut 2·5 cm (1 in) above the surface.

Edging is another important task as the grass starts to grow faster. I do not, as a rule, pick up the trimmings: they quickly dry up and are lost in the soil.

Lawns from seed   From the end of March to the beginning of June is a good time for sowing grass seed (see page 45 for method). If turf is laid during this month, extra care and attention are needed because in dry weather and sunny spells the turf begins to shrink, and topdressing and watering will be required to keep it growing properly.

VEGETABLES

Given reasonable weather and a drying wind there is plenty to keep one busy in the vegetable plot this month.

The first vegetable seeds can be sown and if cloches were put in position in February the soil underneath should have dried out nicely and will be ready for sowings of broad beans, round-seeded peas, parsnips, onions, lettuce and radish.

Make a seed bed at one end of the plot for sowing Brussels sprouts, cauliflower and cabbage now for later transplanting.

Making a seed bed   Sprinkle an organic-based general garden fertiliser over the soil at the rate of a handful to the square yard. Tread the soil in at least two different directions to firm it to ensure there are no air spaces below the surface, also to break down larger lumps and enable the soil to be

Pruning roses

Always remember that the more severely a branch is cut the more vigorous will be the new shoots. Use sharp secateurs and cut to an outward-pointing bud.

First cut out any diseased, weak or badly placed stems to their point of origin and then deal with the main groups as follows: Floribundas (below left) Cut the main branches back halfway, or less if the variety is vigorous. Hybrid tea (below centre) When cutting away dead wood take care not to leave snags, prune back the main branches by a half or, if the plants have been neglected, by two thirds, as shown here. This will encourage strong new growth. Standards (below right) The aim here is to keep the head open and balanced so all crossing and twiggy shoots should be removed and the main branches shortened to half.

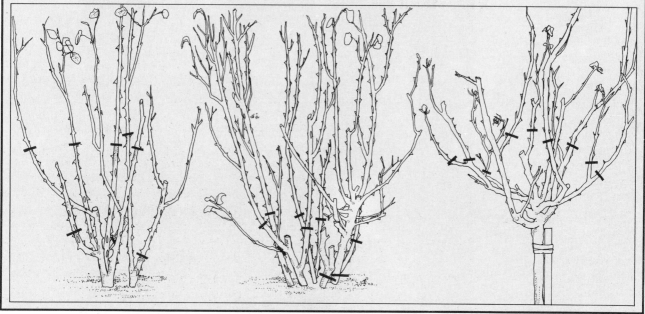

raked down to a fine tilth. A good seed bed is the way to success with all kinds of vegetables.

Planting The peas, broad beans and lettuce sown under glass in February must be properly hardened off to be planted outside towards the end of March and early in April.

Jerusalem artichokes can still be planted, and early potatoes can be put in towards the middle of the month in most parts of the country, though in colder areas they should be left until the end of the month. The variety I choose for the first row is Foremost and this is followed a week or so later by Homeguard or Sharpe's Express. The seed potatoes, which should now be well chitted, should be planted 38 cm (15 in) apart and 10 to 13 cm (4 to 5 in) deep with 60 cm (2 ft) between rows.

It's time enough to plant shallots at the end of the month. Early planting when the soil is cold and wet gives them a check and encourages them to bolt instead of forming bulbs. A similar effect is produced if carrots and beets are sown too early, so if in doubt, wait.

Use a trowel to plant the shallots, placing them 15 cm (6 in) apart in rows 30 cm (12 in) apart and just below the soil surface.

FRUIT

Now is the latest time for planting fruit trees and bushes of all kinds except those which have been container grown—these can be planted at any time, even when producing fruit.

Making a seed bed First tread well.

Rake in several directions.

37

March

Plants of the Month

Signs of spring should now be very noticeable in the garden, with many crocuses in flower and the miniature daffodils coming into bud. The primulas and saxifrages on the rock garden should start to show colour, and shrubs such as *Daphne mezereum* and the various varieties of *Erica carnea* and *E. darleyensis* should still be looking good.

SHRUBS

Chaenomeles (Cydonia, Flowering Quince)
These deciduous shrubs are easily grown in the open, although they can be trained against walls, or even grown as an informal hedge. They are not particular about soil and will grow to between 1 and 2 m (3 and 6 ft) high. The flowers are in shades of red, pink and white and, provided they are not heavily pruned, will be followed in autumn by the quince fruits. If necessary, cut out very old wood after flowering, thin some branches and shorten the side shoots.

Forsythia This well known deciduous shrub is a very welcome sight with its sprays of heavily massed yellow flowers. It will grow anywhere as a specimen shrub, or against a wall, and can be either left unpruned or cut back after flowering if required. Grows to 3 to 3·5 m (10 to 12 ft) high.

Pieris Beautiful evergreen shrub with white, lily-of-the-valley type flowers, which grows to around 2·5 m (8 ft). It requires a lime-free soil and a sheltered position in sun or partial shade. Little pruning is needed. Forrestii is an especially good form with bright red young growth.

Rhododendron praecox Small-growing (to 1·25 m, 4 ft) evergreen shrub with rosy-purple flowers. It requires a lime-free soil and lightly shaded situation. Remove the faded flower heads.

Ribes Deciduous shrub with deep pink flowers, suitable for any soil and situation, and growing to 3 m (10 ft) tall. Some of the older wood can be cut out after flowering. Two of the best varieties are Pulborough Scarlet and King Edward VII.

FLOWERING PLANTS

Anemone blanda (Windflower) Tuberous-rooted plant growing to 15 cm (6 in), with mauve, blue, pink or white flowers in March and April. It requires a well-drained soil, and sunny or lightly shaded sheltered position. Plant in autumn, placing the tubers 5 to 8 cm (2 to 3 in) deep and leave undisturbed.

1 The flowering quince, *Chaenomeles speciosa*
2 Forsythia
3 *Pieris formosa* Forrestii
4 White Splendour, a variety of *Anemone blanda*
5 Scilla

3

4

5

Primula   There are numerous varieties of the lovely primroses and polyanthus, with flowers in shades of pink, red, purple, blue, yellow and white. They grow to about 30 cm (12 in) high and thrive in a shady position and fairly moist soil. Lift and divide after flowering if desired.

Some of the best kinds of primula for the rock garden include *P. edgeworthii, P. marginata* and *P. rosea*. These prefer light, well drained soil and will need to be watered during dry spells in the summer. Those which have downy leaves should be given the protection of a pane of glass in winter. Increase by division in spring.

Saxifraga   Of this large group of rock plants, those which will be coming into flower now belong to the so-called cushion saxifrages. These make hummocks of greyish leaves and produce white, pink or pale yellow flowers on 2·5- to 8-cm (1- to 3-in) stems. Particularly good kinds include Cranbourne, pink; *buseriana*, white or pale yellow; *jenkinsae*, deep pink and Faldonside, yellow.

BULBS

Leucojum (Snowflake)   The spring snowflake, *Leucojum vernum*, is another good bulb for naturalising. It grows to 15 cm (6 in) high and has white, green-tipped flowers. Good for planting in a sunny or shady border or rock garden and needs good fairly moist soil. Leave undisturbed. Flowers may not be produced in the first year.

Narcissus (Daffodil)   The miniature daffodils such as *Narcissus cyclamineus* and *bulbocodium* are suitable for the rock garden. Easily pleased as to soils and position although better in an open sunny site. Plant in late summer or autumn. The same holds good for all the various daffodil and narcissus varieties. Leave undisturbed unless very overcrowded. If naturalised, the grass must be left uncut until the daffodil foliage dies down.

Scilla (Squill)   Bulbs which produce blue, white or lilac flowers slightly reminiscent of the bluebell. Best grown in a sunny position and good sandy soil, and reaching to between 8 and 30 cm (3 and 12 in) high. Plant in autumn, and lift and replant only when overcrowded.

VEGETABLES IN THE GARDEN

Sprouting broccoli, cabbage, winter cauliflower, leeks, lettuce, spring onions, forced rhubarb, leaf beet.

INSIDE

Many of the plants mentioned in previous winter months should still be providing plenty of colour. These include primulas, cinerarias, azaleas and camellias.

March

Inside

When the sun comes out the temperature in the greenhouse is likely to rise rapidly. Open the ventilators on the sheltered side in the middle of the day but close them before the sun goes down.

On sunny days, damp the staging and spray the plants to provide a moist atmosphere.

SOWING

Now is a busy time with much seed sowing to be done. At the beginning of the month sow the annuals for planting out later. These are salvias, antirrhinum (snapdragon), trailing lobelia, ageratum, petunias, *Begonia semperflorens*, large double begonias, gloxinias, streptocarpus, calceolaria and the annual carnations.

All these will need a minimum temperature of 15°C (59°F).

Later in the month the seeds of alyssum, French and African marigolds, nemesia, *Phlox drummondii*, asters, ten-week stocks, nicotiana, salpiglossis and zinnias can be sown.

Because of the high cost of flowers it is much more economical to grow some flowering pot plants and seeds of browallia, *Primula obconica, P. sinensis*, the Pacific strain of polyanthus, and cineraria can all be sown now for winter and spring flowering in the greenhouse.

Any seeds sown in February will need pricking out before they become too crowded and sweet peas sown earlier should be hardened off for planting out as soon as possible.

Vegetable seeds Sow celery, also any tomatoes needed for planting in cool greenhouses

towards the end of next month. I am never anxious to sow tomatoes too early, they do so much better when the days get longer and the sun gains more power. Both these need a temperature of 15°C (59°F) for germination.

If the general temperature can be kept above 15°C (59°F) the tomatoes sown in February can be planted in beds or growing bags.

Begonias and gloxinias Once the tubers have produced prominent shoots they are ready for potting on into 5-in pots using John Innes potting compost No. 2 or a peat-based compost. When potting the begonias I prefer to place the tubers halfway down the pots and cover them with about half-an-inch of compost. This leaves room for topdressing with fresh compost later on. The gloxinias are potted normally with 2·5 cm (1 in) of compost on top.

Where there are three or four shoots on a tuber, these can be divided into pieces

Pricking out Gently lever up the seedlings, handling them with a notched label or by the leaves only. Use a dibber to insert them in another box.

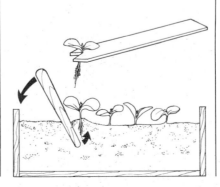

with a shoot on each and each piece can be potted separately. After cutting through the tubers, I find it advisable to dust the cut surface with sulphur or a fungicidal dust to discourage diseases such as botrytis or brown rot from developing.

Carnations Pot on young plants into 5-in pots using John Innes potting compost No. 1 or a peat-based compost, and take out the tips of the plants when they have produced about eight pairs of leaves.

Chrysanthemums It may be necessary to move some of the indoor flowering chrysanthemums out to the garden frame to make more room in the greenhouse.

Take cuttings of the outdoor chrysanthemums as described for the indoor varieties on page 32.

Cyclamen Pot on the young plants sown last June into 4-in pots.

Dahlias Cuttings can be prepared from the boxed up tubers in the same way as chrysanthemum cuttings were taken (page 32).

Fuchsias and geraniums The cuttings taken in the autumn will now need potting on into 5-in pots. The tops should be

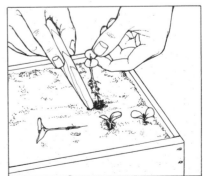

Hanging baskets

A hanging basket makes a most attractive ornamental feature for the garden. In order to give the plants time to grow and cover the basket, it should be planted up this month although, since most of the plants are not hardy, it must be kept indoors until the end of May.

First the basket is lined with moss (black polythene is an alternative lining but some slits must be made in it to allow for drainage), and then filled with a ready mixed potting compost. Those plants such as ivy-leaved pelargoniums and lobelia chosen to trail around the sides are planted first on their sides and then the centre is filled in with upright-growing plants such as fuchsias or geraniums (zonal pelargoniums). Do not overfill with plants as it is important to leave room for growth.

After planting, water well and hang up to drain. Keep watered as required and hang up outside when all danger of frost is past.

removed to encourage side shoots to grow and can then be used for cuttings if required.

Fuchsias stopped earlier should now be making new growths. Pinch out the tip of each shoot when it has produced four to six pairs of leaves.

Cuttings taken in February should be potted singly into 3-in pots using John Innes potting compost No. 1 or a peat-based compost. Pinch out the tips when the plants are 15 cm (6 in) tall.

Schizanthus Feed these and the other spring-flowering annuals weekly.

HOUSE PLANTS

Any rubber trees which have become leggy can be given a new lease of life by air layering.

Make an upward slanting cut about halfway through the stem at a point where you wish the new roots to form.

Dust the cut surfaces with rooting powder and wrap the wounded area with damp moss, pushing some of this up into the cut.

The moss is then bound around with polythene which is sealed around the stem above and below the cut area.

When roots can be seen in the moss the plant is severed from the base and the rooted portion potted. Buds may grow on the lower part of the stem.

CHECK LIST
Make lawn from seed
Plant conifers
Prune spring-flowering
  shrubs
Thin hardy border plants
Plant summer bulbs
Sow hardy annuals
Feed and mow lawn
Plant and sow vegetables
Spray fruit
Make softwood cuttings
Plant tomatoes under glass
Pot house plants

April

'Sweet April showers
do spring May flowers'

I remember my days at school when we used to say
'April showers bring forth May flowers'. No doubt they can
be showers of hail, sleet or snow, but ideally what is needed
are warm showers and sunshine to get things really moving
fast. With these and the soil in a good crumbly state, seed sowing
can begin in earnest.

First consideration should be given to the sowing of hardy
annuals to fill gaps in the borders and provide a long succession
of bright colours throughout the summer months. Some
people like to sow annuals in drills because it makes weeding
easier but I prefer to mark out areas for each variety and then
scatter the seed over the soil and lightly rake them in. There
is an old saying about seed sowing which goes 'One for
the pigeon and one for the crow, One to rot and one to grow'.
There is a lot of truth behind this and the only way to keep
the birds off the seeds is to cover them with nets
or strand cotton across.

Nor are the birds likely to be the only menace in the garden,
slugs can do even more damage and I advise you to keep
on the look out for them especially among vegetables,
rock plants and other creeping ground cover plants. Slug
baits are available and can be very effective but they
should never be scattered over the garden. Instead put them
in small heaps along the sides of the vegetables and around
plants, covering each heap with a flat tile or board propped
up with a small stone. In this way the slugs can get underneath
but birds and domestic animals can't. Also being protected
from the weather they last longer and are more effective.

With the mowing season about to get fully under way
I offer the following advice: always cut round the edge
of the lawn first and round any beds and trees. Then cut
backwards and forwards in straight lines. Never mow grass
or tread on it more than you can help when it is wet.

April

Outside

TREES AND SHRUBS

Planting This is, of course, a good time to plant conifers and other evergreens. Those planted from containers will have a far better chance of survival than those lifted from the nursery and which may have suffered root damage. Ensure the plants are well watered before removing them from their containers; mix peat with the soil as the filling in is done; do not plant too deeply and water after planting if the soil is inclined to be dry.

Pruning Prune forsythias, the flowering currant, ribes, and other spring-flowering shrubs as soon as flowering is is finished. This allows time for the growth of new branches which will mature before winter sets in and provide the flowers next spring. As many of the older branches as possible should be cut right out and many of the younger ones which have flowered should be cut back.

If hebes have been damaged by frost, cut them hard back now.

Erica carnea (winter-flowering heather) and its varieties should now have finished flowering and be ready for trimming back with garden shears or secateurs. The object is to cut off all the flowering shoots, at the same time taking care not to cut back into the hard older wood. After trimming, these will benefit from topdressing with peat.

Where there are weeds growing in between shrubs and other plants, hoe them off or spray them with a paraquat weed-killer. Use the weedkiller with care and store it away from pets and out of reach of children.

FLOWERS

The young shoots of the hardy border plants should be growing well, and those which were not lifted and divided will need to be thinned. It is not wise to leave more than six or seven shoots on plants such as lupins, delphiniums, phlox, heleniums, echinops, Michaelmas daisies and the like. Remove the weakest shoots first and then reduce the remainder.

Should there be some good varieties you want to increase, the shoots must be taken off more carefully just below ground level. These can then be made into cuttings and put into a mixture of peat and sand in pots or boxes.

Plant out the sweet peas towards the end of the month. I do not have time to train them, so I plant them as they are, five or six together in each pot and allow them to climb up over tall pea sticks.

Dahlia tubers can be planted at the same time. Put these in fairly deeply so that the young shoots will not appear until danger of frost has passed.

Feed the hardy border plants now if not done already.

Remove dead flower heads from bulbs to prevent them from producing seed.

Plant the summer-flowering bulbs such as gladioli.

Prepare the ground for the outdoor chrysanthemums and put canes or stakes in position spacing them at least 45 cm (1½ ft) apart.

Sowing annuals Hardy annuals sown from early to mid-April in the open ground will give a good account of themselves from July onwards and make a really fine display.

Popular hardy annuals which can be relied upon are calendula (pot marigold), larkspur, linum (flax), clarkia, linaria, godetia, annual chrysanthemums, bartonia, candytuft, annual lupins, annual lavatera (mallow), cornflowers and nasturtium.

The rock garden Topdress with a mixture of soil, peat and bonemeal if this was not done earlier.

THE LAWN

The making of lawns from seed can continue this month.

Cutting Grass is now growing fast and the lawn is in need of more frequent mowing. The bottom blade of the mower should be lowered slightly so that it is cutting about 1 cm (½ in) above the soil.

The edges of the grass need trimming every time mowing is done and, if done regularly, there will be no need to gather up the trimmings as these soon dry up and are lost in the soil.

Choosing a mower I am often asked about the best kind of mower to use, and my answer is always 'What kind of lawn do you want?'

If it is just a patch of grass for general purposes then a rotary mower is perhaps the ideal. If it is to be a smart, well kept lawn, then it must be a cylinder mower. It is the only one which will give the perfect finish.

Whether it is to be a mower powered by electricity or petrol will depend upon the size of the area of grass to be cut.

Feeding The lawn can be fed now with an all-seasons lawn fertiliser, but if there are daisies, dandelions, plantains, buttercups and other broad-leaved weeds spoiling the appearance, it is better to wait until either the end of this month or May and use a combined lawn fertiliser and selective weed-killer.

VEGETABLES

Those seeds sown under cloches last month should now need thinning out. The cloches can be moved and put over the strawberries.

Hoe between rows to keep down weeds and aerate the soil.
Planting During this month Brussels sprouts, cauliflowers and cabbages sown under glass can be planted out. Give the soil a sprinkling of organic-based general fertiliser at the rate of a handful to the sq m or yd

and tread it well so that it is really firm. Put the plants in 38 cm (15 in) apart and dust the soil around each stem with rootfly dust. As a precaution against club root disease, dip the roots into a paste of calomel dust before planting.

Complete the planting of early potatoes, and early in the month plant onion sets spacing these 23 cm (9 in) apart and just below the soil surface. Main-crop potatoes can be planted towards the end of the month.

There will also be greenhouse sown onions to be planted out, and possibly lettuce and peas if not finished last month.
Sowing Seeds to be sown outdoors now include onions, maincrop carrots, beetroot, parsnips, peas, broad beans, leaf beet, spinach, radish, lettuce, the summer, autumn and Savoy cabbage, winter cauliflower and broccoli.

Before sowing carrots, dust the drills with rootfly dust.
Sow parsley and other herbs.

FRUIT

If raspberries, blackcurrants, strawberries, gooseberries and other fruit were not given fertiliser earlier in the year, then it is another job for this month.

Give attention to pest and disease control and spray pears with a combined insecticide and fungicide before the flowers open.

Spray blackcurrants when the leaves are the size of a tenpenny piece to control big bud mite. Spray gooseberries with fungicide to prevent the beginning of American mildew, and spray strawberries and raspberries with insecticide against aphids and raspberry beetle.

Water all newly planted fruit.

Making a lawn from seed

I always suggest buying the best quality lawn seed—one which does not contain rye grass. The coarser grasses such as rye will eventually seed themselves into the lawn anyway, and in the meantime the finer grasses are easier to maintain.

Prepare the soil thoroughly, removing all weeds, treading to break down lumps and finally raking down to a fine, even surface.

To sow evenly, mark the area into metre- or yard-wide squares using garden lines or canes and then sow at the rate of 40 to 55 g per sq m (1½ to 2 oz per sq yd). After sowing, rake the soil lightly. Use seed treated with a bird repellent or cover the area with nets to keep the birds away until the seed has germinated.

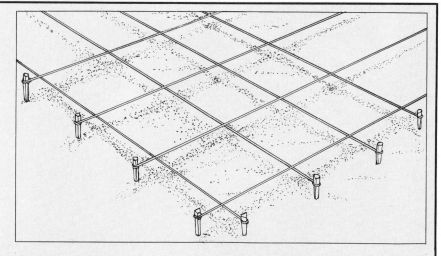

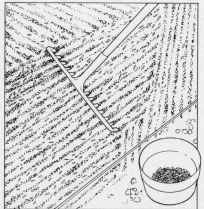

Plants of the Month

This month is notable for bulbs—all of them now very much at their best—and for the rock and alpine plants which will be becoming more colourful each day. Plants that I look forward to seeing in flower on the rock garden are the saxifrages, alpine phlox, antennaria, helianthemum, dianthus, thymus, pulsatilla and cotyledon. This is also the month during which we are likely to see the first of the magnolias in flower.

TREES

Magnolia   Good rich soil and a position in sun or light shade are the requirements of these beautiful trees. The deciduous *Magnolia soulangiana* growing to 6 m (20 ft) and its numerous varieties can all be recommended. Also *M. kobus* and the much smaller *M. stellata*.

No pruning required, but branches can be shortened in summer if necessary.

Malus (Ornamental Crab)   These are beautiful deciduous, spring-flowering trees for any soil and a sunny or open position. Some are grown mainly for the flowers, others for the decorative fruits as well. *Malus floribunda*, the Japanese crab apple, has masses of pink flowers and grows to 7·5 m (25 ft). Varieties especially noted for their colourful late summer fruits are Golden Hornet, bright yellow fruits; John Downie, red and yellow fruits; Red Siberian, red fruits.

SHRUBS AND CLIMBERS

Berberis (Barberry)   The fine evergreen, *Berberis darwinii*, produces its rich orange flowers this month. These will be followed by purple berries. It also makes an excellent hedging plant. It grows to about 2.5 m (8 ft) high and is suited to any soil and, preferably, a sunny position. No pruning required.

Clematis armandii   This climbing plant has large evergreen leaves and small white flowers in April. It succeeds best on good, well drained chalky or limy soils and in a sheltered position, where the top growth can be in sun while the bottom is shaded. Prune after flowering if necessary, thinning and shortening any shoots which require it.

Spiraea (Bridal Wreath)   The deciduous *Spiraea arguta* is smothered in white flowers in April. It will succeed in any soil, but needs plenty of

moisture and an open sunny position, where it will grow to a height of 2 m (6 ft). No pruning required.

FLOWERING PLANTS

Alyssum   The perennial yellow alyssum, *A. saxatile*, is equally good for the rock garden or front of a border, as long as it gets the sunny position and well-drained soil it prefers.

Arabis (Rock Cress)   A white-flowered, trailing perennial which makes an ideal companion for aubrieta, and grows well on sunny walls, rock gardens or banks. There is a variety with cream-variegated leaves which is even more attractive.

Aubrieta   Very popular, trailing perennial plant with flowers in shades of purple, lavender, pink or crimson. It grows well on a sunny rock garden and does best on soils containing lime or chalk, although it will grow elsewhere. Clip over with shears after flowering to encourage new shoots to grow from the base.

Cheiranthus (Wallflowers)   The scented yellow, bronze, orange or crimson flowers of this biennial are a cheerful sight this month. They grow best on well-drained soil, particularly if it contains lime, and in a sunny position.

Doronicum (Leopard's Bane)   Colourful yellow, daisy-like flowers in April and May are the attractions of this herbaceous plant. It is not fussy about soil and is suited to sun or partial shade. Harpur Crewe, 1 m (3 ft) high is the finest variety and there is a shorter one, *Doronicum cordatum*, to only 15 cm (6 in).

Myosotis (Forget-me-not)   A charming biennial plant for any soil and a sunny, open position. Both blue and pink forms are available, and these grow to 15 to 30 cm (6 to 12 in) tall.

Primula   The drumstick primula, *P. denticulata*,

1 *Magnolia soulangiana*
2 A mixed blend of wallflowers planted with forget-me-nots
3 This well planted rock wall features alyssum, aubrieta, tulips and wallflowers
4 *Calceolaria* Covent Garden Strain

will grow anywhere, but prefers a rather damp site. The flowers which grow up to 30 cm (12 in) high are in shades of purple, pink, rose or white. The candelabra primulas, *P. japonica*, *P. pulverulenta* and *P. helodoxa* are best for damp places and grow to 1 m (3 ft). All can be divided and replanted after flowering.

BULBS

Anemone The poppy anemone, *A. coronaria*, makes a good plant for cutting. The flowers, single or double, are in a variety of shades of pink, red, blue and purple in the various strains such as De Caen and St. Brigid. It grows best in a sunny place and good soil. Lift the tubers in August and replant either in autumn or in spring to extend the flowering season.

Fritillaria (Fritillary) The distinctly pendent, bell-shaped flowers are produced in April and May. Some kinds are chequered. Growing to a height of 30 cm to 1 m (1 to 3 ft), they are suited to good soil and an open sunny place. Plant about 8 cm (3 in) deep and leave undisturbed for years.

Muscari (Grape Hyacinth) These little bulbs, with their mauve or deep blue flowers, are ideal for planting on the rock garden or in the front of borders. Plant the bulbs in early autumn placing them 8 cm (3 in) or so deep and about the same distance apart. There is also a white form. Do not distrub unless the clusters are so crowded that flowering suffers. One of the best varieties is Heavenly Blue.

Tulips Together with daffodils, tulips are probably the most popular of the spring-flowering bulbs. They grow well in a light soil and sunny place. The bulbs may be lifted in July when the flowers and leaves have died down, and then replanted in the autumn. Many types and colours are available.

VEGETABLES IN THE GARDEN

Sprouting broccoli, cabbage, cauliflowers, leeks, lettuce, spring onions, rhubarb.

INSIDE

Calceolaria Curious pouch-shaped flowers in bright yellow, red and orange, growing up to 60 cm (2 ft) tall. Numerous varieties are available.
Carnations The perpetual-flowering kinds produce flowers throughout the year for cutting. All colours except blue.

Inside

Keep the ventilators open all day to prevent seedlings from becoming drawn and leggy. Spray the benches and floor with water to maintain a humid atmosphere.

Pricking out   Many seedlings, including the vegetables, will now require pricking out into boxes. After doing this, water the seedlings using a fine rose on the can and then cover them with newspaper for a few days to shade them from the sun.

Sowing   There is still time at the beginning of the month to sow many of the plants listed in March.

Ridge and frame cucumbers, marrows and courgettes can also be sown now if a temperature of 18°C (65°F) can be maintained. I sow two seeds in each 3-in pot and after germination I allow the strongest and best plant to remain and pull out the other. If you have no propagating frame in the greenhouse, I would suggest keeping the pots in the house until the seedlings show above the surface of the compost.

In a cooler temperature— 13°C (55°F)—sweet corn (an excellent variety is First of All) can be sown. Place the seeds individually in peat pots for planting out at the end of May or early June. Now is also the time for sowing seeds of outdoor tomatoes, and for this I use a variety such as Alicante or The Amateur.

Tomatoes   For those with an unheated greenhouse, it should be possible to plant tomatoes now, but if the weather is inclined to be dull and cold, then it is preferable to wait until the end of the month.

Keep an eye on tomatoes already planted in the warm greenhouse, removing any side shoots and feeding the plants, especially if they are in growing bags.

I was always taught that one should not feed tomatoes until the fruits on the first truss are about the size of marbles, but times have changed and now when using growing bags, it is necessary to begin feeding the plants three or four weeks after planting.

Cuttings   Most of the shrubs will now be producing young shoots and these can be used to make softwood cuttings for rooting in a propagating frame.

Bedding plants   By now you should have boxes of half-hardy annuals for summer bedding to be moved from the greenhouse to the garden frame to be hardened off in readiness for planting out at the end of next month. Some of the more hardy kinds will be ready for planting out sooner, these include antirrhinums, penstemons, stocks and asters.

Begonias and gloxinias   These are growing well and the begonias are ready for a top-dressing of John Innes potting compost No. 3 or a peat-based compost.

Chrysanthemums   Remove the tips from the indoor flowering chrysanthemums when they have formed six or seven leaves. I grow only the Favourite varieties for flowering from late November to January. They are the easiest for the average greenhouse and have a wide range of colours—white, pink, red, bronze and yellow. Pot on individual plants into 5-in

Taking softwood cuttings Select pieces of soft new growth. Trim the ends and insert in a pot. Root in a propagating frame, or a plastic bag if only a small quantity is involved.

pots and John Innes compost No. 2.

Harden off the outdoor varieties for planting out next month.

Fuchsias   Pot up any rooted

Potting

When plants fill their existing pots with roots—a condition known as potbound—they will need to be potted on into larger pots. Lack of new growth or the appearance of roots through the holes in the bottom of the pot are indications that the plant has reached this state.

An hour or so before potting it is important to water the plant well so that the rootball is thoroughly moistened. Remove the plant from its pot by up-turning it and giving the rim of the pot a sharp knock against a hard surface. The new pot should be about an inch bigger than the existing one, although some of the more rapidly growing plants such as chrysanthemum may be put into pots up to two inches larger.

Place some potting compost in the bottom of a clean pot and then position the rootball so that it is between 1 and 2·5 cm ($\frac{1}{2}$ and 1 in) below the rim of the new pot depending on its size. Fill in between the rootball and pot with more compost and firm with the fingers. The soilless potting composts do not require as much firming as the soil-based ones. Finally, water again to settle the compost around the roots. Keep the plants for a few days in shade.

When potting plants, and especially house plants, do not use ordinary garden soil which may well contain pests and diseases. Instead use one of the proprietary ready-mixed composts.

cuttings into 3-in pots.

The fuchsias which are wanted for large specimen plants should now be ready for moving on into larger pots and John Innes potting compost No. 3.

Any plants with dry soil must be throughly watered an hour or so before potting; to pot plants on when compost around the roots is dry can prove fatal, and any water given after potting will drain quickly through the new compost.

The tips should be pinched out again.

HOUSE PLANTS

Many of these will now be ready for repotting and those in very large pots which cannot be repotted should have the top inch or so of compost replaced with fresh.

Pot up all well rooted cuttings.

CHECK LIST
Prune shrubs
Spray roses
Weed
Plant water plants
Lift bulbs
Spray fruit
Harden off seedlings
Sow runner beans
Plant cucumbers

May

'A wet and windy May
fills the barns
with corn and hay'

Now we are into May, let us hope that we have seen the last
of night frosts. More than a few degrees at this time of year
can do untold damage. Over the years I have seen the young
leaves on oak and sycamore trees completely browned by severe
frost and looking as though they had been burnt.

The possibility of late frosts occurring, however, must always
be borne in mind. No matter how warm the weather is in early
May it would be unwise to get carried away and plant
out the tender vegetables and other plants too early.

The important job this month is to begin the hardening off
of all the bedding plants to be planted out at the end of May
or early in June. Bedding is the word used to describe
the plants that are put in to create an effect over a particular season
but are not permanent features of the garden. Most of the plants
used for bedding are annuals and biennials or perennials
which are killed by frost and so cannot be left out throughout
the year. If you have a greenhouse or conservatory then it is
very satisfying to grow these plants for yourself from seed.
If you don't grow them then they can be bought in boxes or pots
from a garden centre or local nursery.

When buying bedding plants there are a few points
to be taken into consideration. First, with some exceptions,
it is unwise to buy plants until the last week of May, when
you can be almost sure that it is too late for the severe
frosts which would be likely to kill them. The exceptions include
penstemons, violas, pansies, antirrhinums, stocks and asters.

When buying, choose plants that are short jointed and sturdy
and with foliage of a good dark green. If the stems are thin
and drawn it shows that the plants have been weakened
by too much heat or too little light. When it comes to planting,
soak the box or pots of plants well and water the soil in the bed
if it is very dry. Make a hole with a trowel and plant firmly
pressing the soil well into contact with the plant's roots.
Pinch out the growing tip from each plant to encourage it
to produce side shoots, all of which should bear flowers.
Do the planting in the late afternoon or evenings if possible.

51

Outside

TREES AND SHRUBS

Pruning   There is often considerable confusion about the pruning of shrubs. Many which flower at this time of year need to be pruned after flowering. Brooms are now coming into flower, and if left unpruned for a number of years they will become large, untidy and their lifetime will be shortened. Remove the shoots which have just flowered, but do not cut into the older wood.

Escallonias and weigelas will also need pruning, and again I cut out as many as possible of the branches which have just flowered.

Prune the early-flowering clematis, cutting it back to fill the space available and removing old and poor growth.

Spraying roses   Spraying is one of the few jobs I do not like doing, but it is necessary if the plants are to be kept free from pests and diseases; roses in particular will need regular spraying at this time of the year. For this I use an insecticide to which a fungicide has been added to make a combined spray which will be effective against greenfly and diseases such as mildew and black spot.

When spraying roses, check and treat other plants, such as the clematis, if necessary.

Weed control   Weeds seem to grow faster than any other plants at this time of the year, and the secret of a weed-free garden is to eradicate the weeds before they have the opportunity to produce seeds. A paraquat-based weedkiller is very useful for controlling the weeds between the roses, shrubs, and under the hedges. Paraquat is quickly absorbed by weeds and becomes inactive on touching the soil.

The paths and drives will need to be treated with a special weedkiller which will last two or three months, killing the current crop of weeds and preventing further weed seed germinations.

FLOWERS

Continue to thin the shoots of the hardy border plants as described in April. Stake the flower spikes as they develop, paying particular attention to delphiniums and lupins.

Polyanthus are now coming to the end of their flowering and they can be lifted, divided and planted in a partially shaded part of the garden to make good plants for going back into the beds and borders in the autumn.

Continue to dead head the daffodils. It is also as well to remember that narcissus fly is an insect pest which is active at this time of year. It lays eggs at the base of the stems or on the soil nearby and prevents the bulbs from forming new flowers. If you have daffodil bulbs which have not flowered, dust the soil or grass around the base of the leaves with a rootfly dust.

Clear away the spring bedding plants such as wallflowers and forget-me-nots. Lift bulbs and heel them in in another part of the garden, leaving them there until the leaves die back before lifting, drying and storing them away for autumn planting.

Thin hardy annuals as necessary, and towards the middle of the month sow the half-hardy annuals in the garden if you have been unable to do this in a greenhouse.

Sowing   Towards the end of the month the biennials such as wallflowers, Sweet Williams and Canterbury bells should be sown in the northern parts of the country.

There can be a great saving in growing your own hardy border plants and rock plants from seed. These can be sown now in a seed bed.

Planting   Plant the outdoor chrysanthemums, placing each one by a stake and firming it in well. The centre tips should be removed about a week later.

Above Planting out a young chrysanthemum plant. *Below* A week or so later the tip is removed.

Towards the end of the month the rooted dahlia cuttings can also be planted. Dahlias like a good, well worked soil to which some garden compost or decayed manure has been added.

Early in the month it should be safe to plant out more hardy types of plants raised under glass. These will include penstemons, violas, pansies, antirrhinums, stocks and asters.

THE LAWN

Continue mowing regularly.

This is a good time to use a selective weedkiller with an added lawn fertiliser to control the majority of the broad-leaved weeds. Speedwell and yellow suckling clover are more difficult to control and need a special weedkiller based on morfamquat. All weedkillers should be used when the weather is dry and still.

VEGETABLES

Keep the hoe going among the vegetables to keep down the weeds, and thin those crops that need it.

Prepare the ground for runner beans early in the month, digging the soil well and incorporating manure or garden compost. Put the supporting canes, string or nets in position.

Earth up early potatoes as the shoots show through the soil.

Sowing   Continue to sow in succession the salad crops, broad beans and also more peas, carrots, parsnips, leaf beet and some broccoli. Other sowings include the winter and savoy cabbages, spinach, turnips and swedes.

Towards the middle of the month, runner and French beans, marrows, ridge cucumbers and sweet corn and courgettes can be sown out of doors and it is a good idea

Planting water plants

It is advisable to have a range of depths available in the pool to allow for the planting of the various types of water plants. Some, such as reed mace, flowering rush and kingcup required only 8 cm (3 in) or so of water, whilst the water lilies and other aquatics with floating

flowers and leaves need from 20 cm to 1 m (8 in to 3 ft) depending on variety.

Water lilies and marginal plants are best planted in special plastic baskets. Use good soil to which some bonemeal has been added and finish off with a layer of gravel.

If you intend to keep fish some oxygenating plants should be included.

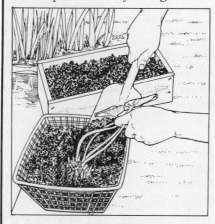
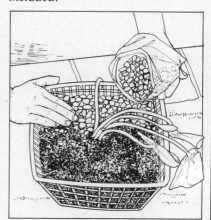
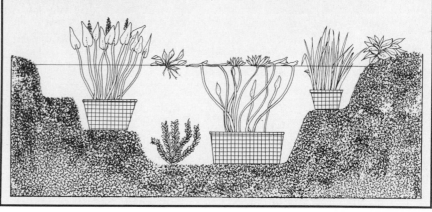

to move the cloches from the strawberries and use them on these sowings until they are established.

Planting   Start to transplant Brussels sprouts, broccoli, cabbage and cauliflowers from the seed bed, spacing these well apart (see page 45), and dipping the roots in calomel paste as described last month.

Plant self-blanching celery 23 cm (9 in) apart and at the end of the month plant the outdoor tomatoes spacing these 45 cm (1½ ft) apart.

FRUIT

Spray apples when the buds are showing pink with a combined insecticide and fungicide to control apple scab, and the grubs of sawfly and winter moth.

Start to thin the young shoots of the raspberries as these show through the ground. They should be spaced about 23 cm (9 in) apart.

Put straw or black polythene around the strawberries and place nets over the plants to protect the ripening fruits from the birds.

May

Plants of the Month

There are so many good plants coming into flower it is difficult to make a selection. To think of May is to think of the azaleas and rhododendrons, the flowering cherries and laburnum, as well as the lovely border plants such as the peony and the bearded or flag iris.

TREES

Laburnum   A group of deciduous trees which grow to a height of 6 m (20 ft) and produce yellow flowers in May and June. They will succeed in most soils but do best in an open position. No pruning required. It is important to note that the seeds are poisonous and will prove a problem with pets, and especially with children.

Prunus (Flowering Cherries)   Magnificent range of easily grown trees for almost any soil and position and suited to a chalky or limy soil. No regular pruning needed, but diseased or damaged branches should be removed immediately after flowering and the wounds painted with a bituminous paint. The large-flowered Japanese cherries are the most spectacular and some, such as *Prunus sargentii*, have good autumn colour. Height range 2 to 7·5 m (6 to 25 ft) according to variety.

SHRUBS and CLIMBERS

Ceanothus (Californian lilac)   It is the evergreen varieties which produce their blue flowers at this time of year. All varieties appreciate a well-drained soil and need the shelter of a sunny wall. Prune lightly after flowering to keep them in shape. Good species include *Ceanothus burkwoodii* and *C. thyrsiflorus*.

Clematis   For a chalky or limy soil and a sunny wall, few climbing plants give faster coverage than *Clematis montana*, which also produces masses of pink or white flowers in May. Prune after flowering if required.

Genista (Spanish Gorse)   *Genista hispanica* is a dwarf species spreading to 60 cm (2 ft). Like other genistas, it requires sun and good drainage; this species grows well on a rock garden. Prune after flowering, but do not cut into old hard wood.

Helianthemum (Sun Rose)   Bushy plants growing to 30 cm (12 in) high and good for planting on a rock garden or dry wall, and producing vividly coloured flowers in shades of yellow, copper,

pink and crimson as well as white. Lightly clip with the shears after flowering.

Rhododendron   The deciduous kinds are commonly known as azaleas, the evergreen kinds as rhododendrons. They are suited to most soils which do not contain chalk, and a lightly shaded position. Remove the faded flowers to prevent seed pods forming. There are many species and a wide range of varieties growing from prostrate to 6 m (20 ft) in height.

Weigela   Also known as diervilla, these pink- or crimson-flowering deciduous shrubs are easily grown in almost any soil and position. One which is especially worth growing is *Weigela florida variegata* with pink flowers and cream-edged leaves. Height 2 to 2·5 m (6 to 7 ft). The flowering stems can be cut back to non-flowering shoots as soon as the flowers fade to restrict the size of the plant.

Euphorbia (Spurge)   These hardy border plants are grown mainly for their decorative foliage and striking heads of leafy bracts, and succeed best in well drained soils and a sunny place. *Euphorbia griffithii* has reddish-orange bracts and *E. wulfenii* has large heads of greenish-yellow bracts. Height varies with species up to 1·5 m (5 ft).

Geranium   Quite different from the bedding geraniums, these plants will grow in any soil and open position. Varieties range in height from prostrate to 1 m (3 ft), and flowers in colour from white to pink, blue and magenta. Typical species are *Geranium grandiflorum* and *G. endressii*.

Paeonia (Peony)   There are many varieties of this border plant growing about 1 m (3 ft) high with flowers ranging in colour from white, yellow through to deep red. They succeed best in deep rich soils and a sunny or partially shaded position Do not disturb after planting.

BULBS

Ornithogalum (Star of Bethlehem)   Growing to about 30 cm (1 ft) high with loose sprays of white flowers, ornithogalums will grow in almost any soil in an open sunny situation. Leave undisturbed until overcrowded.

VEGETABLES IN THE GARDEN

Cabbage, kale, lettuce, spring onions, radish, rhubarb, spinach.

FRUIT IN THE GARDEN

Gooseberry (culinary).

INSIDE

Regal pelargoniums   These form one group of the familiar greenhouse geranium. The flowers, in a wide range of pinks, purples and white, are often blotched with one colour on another. May to June is the main flowering period.

Schizanthus (Butterfly Flower)   Bushy plants up to 1·25 m (4 ft) tall with spikes of flowers in many colours.

Wisteria   One of the most beautiful of all climbers with trailing flowers of blue, mauve, pink or white in May and June. They will succeed in most good soils and a sunny place. Shorten the side shoots to four or five leaves after flowering and cut back further to 5 or 8 cm (2 or 3 in).

FLOWERING PLANTS

Convallaria (Lily of the Valley)   Hardy border plant to 23 cm (9 in) tall, with scented flowers and growing best in a cool shady place and rich moist soils. It can be forced into flower early in the greenhouse.

Digitalis (Foxglove)   Best in a cool, shady place and moist soil, foxgloves spread rapidly by self-sown seed. The Excelsior varieties have larger flowers than the wild kinds, and all grow to 1 to 1·5 m (3 to 5 ft) tall. Usually grown as biennials.

May

Inside

Watering must be attended to regularly now that the temperature outside is rising. When watering with a can, hold the spout close to the soil so as not to splash the water over the plants or disturb the soil unduly. Before giving water to any plant, examine the surface of the compost to see if this is dry, and feel the weight of the pot itself. With a little practice you will soon be able to tell if watering is required.

Some form of shading will be needed on the house for use on very bright days. This can be either a permanent form in the way of blinds or the more temporary whitewash which is painted on the outside.

Bedding plants There are now many pots and boxes of bedding plants to be moved out of the greenhouse to the garden frame to be hardened off gradually. If frost is forecast, or if there is that all-too-familiar nip in the air in the evening, the frame lights will certainly have to be put back on. It only takes a few degrees of frost to spoil the appearance of the plants by browning the young shoots and tips of the leaves.

Some of the boxes may have to be placed under the shelter of the side of the greenhouse if there is not sufficient space in the frame. In the event of threatening frost these should be covered with layers of either newspaper or some light material.

VEGETABLES

As well as bedding plants to be hardened off, there are boxes of celery and leeks and pots of marrows, courgettes, cucumbers, and sweet corn.

During the early part of the month sow some runner beans in peat pots for planting out early in June. I grow half my runner beans in this way, the other half being sown in the open ground around mid-May. I also make a point of sowing a short row in the open ground in early June so that, if the autumn weather is mild, it is possible to pick runner beans as late as October.

Tomatoes in the warm greenhouse should now be growing well and the first fruits beginning to form. The plants which are in growing bags will need much more watering and feeding.

Hardening off is the process by which plants raised in a greenhouse are accustomed gradually to outdoor temperatures. The boxes are placed in a frame and the frame light is opened by steadily increasing amounts during the day until it is left off altogether—first during the day and then at night as well.

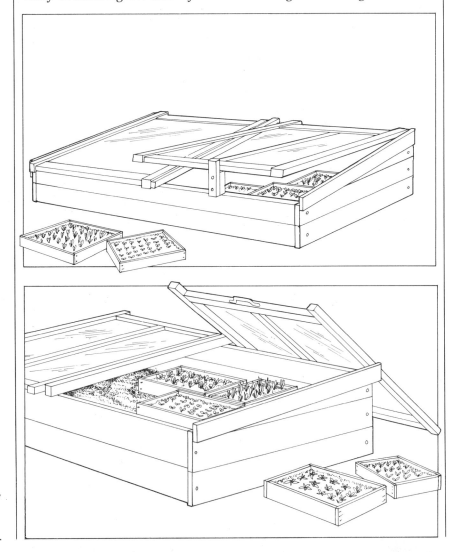

56

Early in May, the seedlings of the frame cucumbers can be planted in the greenhouse on mounds of well-rotted manure or garden compost covered with John Innes potting compost No. 3 or one of the peat-based composts. Each plant should be given a cane to support the main stem, and the side shoots should be trained along horizontal wires stretched along the greenhouse at intervals of 38 cm (15 in). The plants can be allowed to grow to the top of the greenhouse before the tips are pinched out. In the meantime, as side shoots grow, the tip of each should be pinched out at the second leaf.

On cucumbers the female flowers normally form at the first leaf joint. Remove all male flowers as soon as they appear because pollination of the female flowers will result in bitter bulb-ended fruits.

Once the bedding plants have been removed from the frame this can also be used to grow cucumbers.

FLOWERS

Continue to prick out seedlings of primroses and other plants for greenhouse flowering and pot these on when necessary into 3½-in pots. Sow *Primula malacoides* for winter flowering.

Towards the middle of the month cinerarias and large-flowered hybrid calceolarias can be sown. The cinerarias will flower from January to April in the following year, and the calceolarias from April to June.

Pots of fuchsias and geraniums will need a lot of water from now on and will also benefit from a weekly feed with liquid fertiliser.

Take geranium cuttings as previously described (page 32) to provide winter-flowering plants.

Fuchsia cuttings taken in March are now moved on from 3-in to 5-in pots.

Stake and tie in the growths of perpetual-flowering carnations.

Feed tuberous begonias and pot on those grown from seed.

Begonia semperflorens is a marvellous bedding plant and this can be set out at the end of May.

Gradually dry off the old cyclamen corms.

Hanging baskets The plants should now have filled the compost in the baskets and will benefit from feeding weekly with liquid fertiliser. These can be hung out of doors at the end of the month.

HOUSE PLANTS

Continue to repot where necessary. Feed all plants every ten days or so with a liquid fertiliser.

The young cucumber plants are set out in the greenhouse on mounds of soil or well-rotted manure.

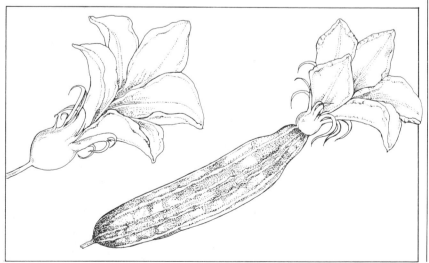

Unless an all-female variety of cucumber is being grown, it is necessary to remove the male flower (far left) to prevent pollination taking place. The female flower can be recognised by the presence of an embryo fruit behind the petals (near left).

June

'A dripping June
keeps all in tune'

Although we always hope to see a hot, sunny June, with our variable climate this is not always the case. However, should the weather turn out to be dry then the gardening job which should be at the top of the list now is watering. Plants are growing rapidly and need both water and food if they are to give of their best and I always think it is better to water too much than too little. Heavy rain, too, may often be deceptive as it frequently runs off the soil surface without reaching the plant's roots. Thorough, gentle watering is what is needed, using either a sprinkler or a hose pipe fitted with an adjustable nozzle. If water restrictions are in force then use whatever water is available—from butts or the waste from household tasks—on the plants which need it most: the vegetables such as lettuce, beans and celery, newly planted seedlings and anything growing in containers, window boxes and pots. Tub-grown plants are especially vulnerable to lack of water and will quickly die.

If you haven't already done so, now is the time to mulch fruit crops and border plants, too, if a sufficient quantity of organic matter is available. To mulch simply means to spread a layer of garden compost, composted bark, peat or decayed manure to a depth of several inches over the area of the plant's roots, being careful to keep manure away from the stem. This helps to conserve moisture, keeps the warmth in the soil and, in the case of fruit trees, encourages the fruits to swell. Strips of black polythene can be used for the same purpose, although these don't add any food value to the soil.

With the warmer weather, there is always an increase in pests and diseases, so be on the look out for greenfly, blackfly and mildew and black spot on roses. I am a great believer in prevention being better than cure and this is why I make a point of spraying early in the year to stop the insects or diseases gaining a hold. When applying sprays always read and follow the maker's instructions.

CHECK LIST

Plant bedding plants
Water
Cut back rock plants
Lift and divide iris
Sow spring - flowering biennials
Plant vegetables
Mulch strawberries
Train cucumbers
Stand house plants outdoors
Shade greenhouse
Pot chrysanthemums

June

Outside

TREES AND SHRUBS

Pruning Continue to prune the early-flowering shrubs. Those such as lilac and rhododendron which flower on the tips of the branches rarely need pruning, but if they get leggy they can be cut back into shape after flowering.

As soon as flowering is finished, make a point of breaking off the fading and dead flowers from azaleas and rhododendrons. By removing these before the seedpods form, the growth of the young shoots which produce next year's flowers will be stimulated.

Spraying Honeysuckle often suffers crippling attacks of blackfly. Spray now with a systemic insecticide and treat clematis as well against greenfly.

While the spray is in use treat roses again with a combined fungicide and insecticide.

I always prefer to do the spraying in the evening and not when the sun is shining because this can cause leaf scorch. Also, in the evenings there is less likelihood of doing damage to the bees. Use a fine forceful spray to ensure a thorough wetting of the leaves and stems.

Roses Keep an eye on the roses for the first signs of any suckers growing from the rootstocks. These differ markedly from the rest of the plant in having more leaflets and thorns. If left to grow they will weaken the plant. Clear away the soil and cut or pull the suckers away from the point of origin.

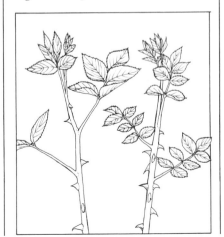

Rose sucker (on right of picture) has more thorns and leaves.

FLOWERS

Planting the bedding plants
Prepare the soil well by digging and putting on a dressing of general garden fertiliser. Water the plants before removing them from their pots or boxes and space them so that each has room to grow and develop. Water in thoroughly after planting.

In the event of there being a few days of dry warm weather, these plants will need watering again to help them get established and begin their flowering. Our summer season is short enough anyway, and the sooner they begin to flower the better.

If it is necessary to water the plants, I like to hoe between them the following day to prevent the cracking of the surface soil and thereby the loss of moisture from the soil.

Containers The best plants for pots, troughs and other containers are fuchsias, geraniums, trailing lobelia, petunias and *Begonia semperflorens*.

When planting up the containers it is important to use a good compost such as John Innes potting compost No. 3, and not ordinary garden soil.

Make sure the drainage holes are clear and put a layer of broken crocks at the base of each container. Containers hold a large number of plants in a small rooting area, so it is important to remember that they need regular watering once a day, every day. Feed once a week by adding a liquid fertiliser to the water.

Regular watering is particularly important for hanging

Planting bedding plants *Above* Separate plants carefully. *Below* Make a hole deep enough for the roots and then firm well.

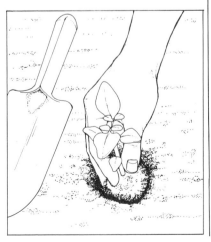

60

baskets which are exposed to winds and sun and reflected heat from buildings. These may even need watering twice a day.

Flowering annuals There are many annuals which can still be sown for flowering during the latter part of the summer. These include cornflower, godetia, clarkia, annual chrysanthemum, eschscholzia, poppies, candytuft and dwarf nasturtiums. It is not too late either to sprinkle the seed of the night-scented stock in various parts of the garden.

Spring-flowering biennials With the summer bedding now completed we must turn our minds to preparations for the spring of next year. And now is the time for sowing seed of wallflowers, forget-me-nots, bellis, Sweet William, Canterbury bells and foxgloves, so that the plants will be large enough for planting out in the autumn.

Of the many wallflower varieties I prefer to grow Persian Carpet which includes a range of mostly pastel shades. *Myosotis* Dwarf Blue is, I consider, one of the best forget-me-nots and ideal for planting in between tulips. Bellis is often listed in catalogues under daisy, and I find Double Carpet Mixed is a good all round mixture.

Sow all of these in a seed bed out of doors, making shallow drills and sprinkling the seed thinly. If the soil is dry, water along the drills before sowing.

General plant care Do not allow sweet peas to dry out, and feed regularly with a general fertiliser.

Stake gladiolus spikes as these start to form.

Remove seed pods from lupins and delphiniums as soon as the flowers fade. This encourages a second crop in July or August.

If they are overcrowded, lift and divide bearded iris (once called the flag iris) when they

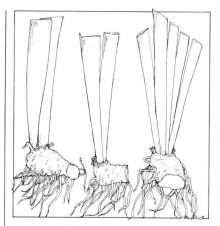
Trimmed iris rhizome.

finish flowering. Select firm young pieces of rhizome and discard the older pieces from the centre. Cut back the leaves to 23 cm (9 in) to prevent windrock. Plant so that the top of the rhizome just shows above the soil.

Chrysanthemums must be stopped by removing the centre tip of each plant if this was not done last month. This encourages side shoots to grow which will flower from late August onwards.

Dahlias recently planted and grown from cuttings will be better for stopping too if this has not been done. The flowers of these plants, like those of chrysanthemums, will benefit from watering if the weather is dry to ensure they establish themselves as quickly as possible.

Areas where daffodils have been flowering may be looking untidy with dead leaves falling over the uncut long grass. My teaching has always been not to cut the grass and disturb the leaves until they die down naturally. However, the Royal Horticultural Society has been carrying out experiments for the past few years at their garden at Wisley, and it has been found that if leaves are cut off six to seven weeks after flowering there is little or no detrimental effect on the flowering of the bulbs the following years.

It should, in the normal course of events, be possible to cut the long grass where bulbs have been naturalised by the end of June.

The rock garden A lot of plants may have outgrown their allotted space and should be cut back to keep the rock garden looking neat and tidy. As soon as they finish flowering go over them with shears or secateurs: most likely to need this treatment are alyssum, alpine phlox, aubrieta, helianthemum and dianthus. Cutting back will encourage the plants to produce new shoots from the base which will make ideal cuttings.

Using shears, trim over rock plants to tidy them up, removing dead flowers and encouraging new growth.

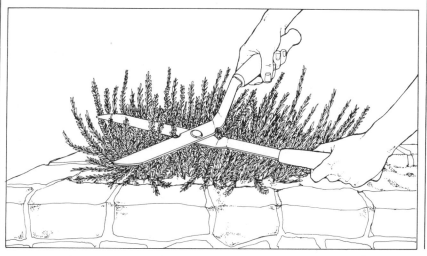

June

Plants of the Month

Glorious June brings so much colour and richness to the garden in a wealth of wonderful plants, that in making any selection, it is inevitable that many worthwhile kinds are left out.

TREES

Robinia pseudoacacia (False Acacia)
Deciduous tree with a preference for well-drained soil and a sunny position. There is an especially fine form with brilliant yellow leaves called Frisia. Prune if necessary to restrict size in autumn or late winter.

SHRUBS and CLIMBERS

Cistus (Rock Rose)   Thriving in a sunny position and well-drained soil, the lovely evergreen cistus produce their white, pink or magenta flowers in June and July. Average height around 1 m (3 ft). No regular pruning required.

Lonicera (Honeysuckle)   These evergreen and deciduous climbers will succeed in reasonably good soil and sun or partial shade. The flowers are fragrant, and cream, yellow, orange or red in colour according to species. Remove some of the older stems after flowering.

Philadelphus (Mock Orange)   Mostly with highly scented white flowers, these shrubs grow from 1 to 4·5 m (3 to 15 ft) depending on variety. They are suited to any soil but, for preference, a sunny position. Prune after flowering, cutting out the old flowering stems.

Potentilla (Cinquefoil)   There are several very low-growing species, but the most widely grown are the shrubby varieties which are between 60 cm and 1·25 m (2 and 4 ft) tall. All are suited to well drained soil and a sunny position and flower from June to September. Prune in spring, either simply thinning out some of the older stems or cutting everything back to within a few inches of the ground.

Syringa (Lilac)   Deciduous shrubs and trees growing to 4·5 m (15 ft) high in any soil and reasonably open place. The sweetly scented flowers range from white through mauve to deep purple according to variety. Remove all suckers. After flowering, cut out weaker shoots and spent flowers.

FLOWERING PLANTS

Achillea (Yarrow)   Growing up to 1·25 m

1 *Cistus purpureus*, a beautiful but slightly tender hybrid of the rock rose
2 *Lonicera americana*, a deciduous form of honeysuckle
3 Canterbury bells, *Campanula medium*
4 Iceland poppies, *Papaver nudicaule*
5 A well stocked vegetable garden

(4 ft) tall, with flat clusters of white, yellow or pink flowers, the perennial yarrows are very hardy and easily pleased. The grey-foliaged varieties like well drained soil and a sunny place; the other kinds will grow anywhere.

Campanula (Canterbury Bells)   The biennial *Campanula medium* is grown as a summer bedding plant and does best in a sunny position and good soil. Reaching a height of about 1 m (3 ft) it produces large cup-and-saucer-type flowers in shades of blue, mauve, pink and white.

Dianthus (Sweet William)   These charming plants with their flattish heads of scented flowers appearing in June, are usually grown as biennials, although they will sometimes survive for several years. They range in height from 15 to 45 cm (6 to 18 in) and will grow in almost any soil, with a preference for the well drained.

Iris   The herbaceous bearded or flag irises grow to 1·25 m (4 ft) and have a very wide range of flower colours. They will succeed in any soil and sunny place, but prefer a chalky soil.

Lupin   Growing well in most kinds of soil, especially the sandy, well-drained types, and an open situation, the perennial lupins come in all colours and reach a height of about 1·25 m (4 ft). The Russell lupins are the finest form. None are very long lived and are best renewed from seed.

Papaver (Poppy)   All poppies require a sunny position and well drained soil. The oriental poppy, *Papaver orientale*, is particularly fine with large pink, red or white flowers on 1 m (3 ft) stems. Coming in with a range of yellow, orange or white flowers is the Iceland poppy, *P. nudicaule*, which is usually grown as an annual or biennial.

BULBS

Allium (Ornamental Onions)   There are many species and varieties, ranging in height from 23 cm to 1·25 m (9 in to 4 ft). All are suited to a sunny position and ordinary soil, and produce globular heads of white, yellow, purple or blue flowers. Good summer-flowering kinds include *Allium albopilosum*, *A. giganteum* and *A. caeruleum*.

VEGETABLES IN THE GARDEN

Broad beans, cabbage, carrots, cauliflower, lettuce, spring onions, onions (sown August or September), peas, early potatoes, radish, rhubarb, spinach, turnips. Tomatoes in the greenhouse.

FRUIT IN THE GARDEN

Cherry (early varieties), gooseberries, raspberries and strawberries.

INSIDE

Geranium (Zonal pelargonium)   This is one of the most popular of all bedding plants with colourful heads of flowers produced over a long season. Some varieties have leaves marked with rings or zones of other colours.

Streptocarpus (Cape Primrose)   Trumpet-shaped flowers in blue, pink, red or white, which are produced in summer or early autumn on 30 to 45 cm (12 to 18 in) long stems.

THE LAWN

In periods of dry weather the grass soon begins to scorch, so if we can water the lawn it will help to keep it a lush green colour.

This is a time for a regular weekly mowing with the bottom blade set at 1 cm ($\frac{1}{2}$ in) above the level of the soil.

VEGETABLES

Sowing In the vegetable garden there is more lettuce, radish, leaf beat, spinach, carrots, turnips and peas to sow to ensure a continuity of supply.

I like to make another sowing of runner beans in the first week of June to provide later supplies. Those sown last month and planted out at the beginning of this month should soon be growing well, and a few plants may need tying in to get them to grow up the cane provided, rather than encroaching on those adjoining. If there are spells of dry weather, water the beans at regular intervals, and when flowers begin to form spray them overhead with water to assist in the setting.

Planting out The celery sown under glass should now be planted. I put mine in a single row in a trench, 38 cm (15 in) wide, and no more than 15 to 20 cm (6 to 8 in) deep, spacing the plants 30 cm (12 in) apart along the trench. These will need good watering after planting and again in a few days if the weather remains dry.

To help get the plants off to a good start, before planting sprinkle some organic-based general fertiliser along the trench at the rate of a handful to the metre (yard) row.

I plant half the trench with white celery, which has to be used first, and the remaining half with pink or red which is more hardy and will stand into late December or even January.

Leeks should also be ready for planting out and these I plant with a dibber, making a hole 15 to 20 cm (6 to 8 in) deep and dropping one plant in each hole. Fill each hole with water and this will carry sufficient soil down to cover the roots. The tips of the leek leaves can just be seen above the soil. Space them 30 cm (12 in) apart, with 38 to 45 cm (15 to 18 in) between the rows.

The marrows, courgettes, cucumbers and sweet corn sown in individual pots can also be planted now.

Ridge cucumbers are planted on mounds of soil which has been well mixed with garden compost or manure.

Planting of Brussels sprouts must be finished as soon as possible. Dip the roots in a paste of calomel dust and water as a preventive measure against club root, and dust the soil around plants with rootfly dust. Water well after planting.

General cultivation Remove tips from early broad bean plants to encourage pods to form and prevent black fly damage.

Spray French and runner beans against blackfly.

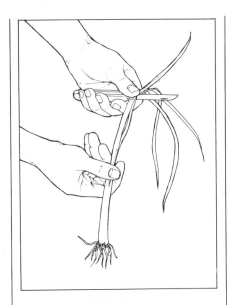

Above and below Planting leeks. Trim the leaves and drop each plant in a hole.

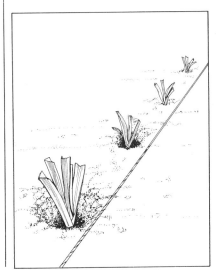

Below Setting out celery plants.

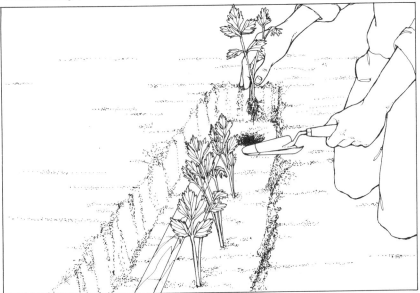

Turn some of the inner leaves down over the developing curds of cauliflower.

Earth up maincrop potatoes. Towards the end of the month you may be able to lift early potatoes. Try one plant just to see what size the tubers are.

Remove any flower spikes which form on rhubarb. Water and feed plants and topdress with garden compost.

FRUIT

The outdoor strawberries are now in need of straw or matting to keep the fruit off the soil and prevent them becoming gritty. Place nets over them to keep the birds away.

Strawberry and raspberry picking should be in full swing by the end of the month. At the beginning of June, raspberries should be sprayed with derris to control the grubs of the raspberry beetle.

Spray plums and cherries with an insecticide; if grown as wall-trained specimens they should be netted against attacks by birds.

Keep a watch on gooseberries and spray against mildew with dinocap if necessary. Pick the first fruits and use for cooking, leaving the remaining ones to make dessert fruit for later use.

Tie the brittle young shoots of blackberries and loganberries into the supporting wires.

Watering

During the summer months watering should be given priority if the weather is dry. But it must be done properly—a sprinkling which does little more than damp the surface does more harm than good since it encourages the plants to send their roots to the surface where they are much more vulnerable to prolonged periods of drought. Thorough, gentle watering is what is needed and this is provided most easily by the use of a sprinkler attached to a hose.

There are two main kinds of sprinklers: the oscillating and the rotary, the difference between them being in the shape and sizes of the area they water, the oscillating covering a rectangular- or square-shaped area and the rotary a circular area.

Some hosepipes have holes all along their length which also allow large areas to be watered at the same time. Watering with a hose only is made easier by the use of a nozzle attachment to break the force of the spray. Heavy deluges of water are never as effective as they tend to break down the soil structure and cause compaction.

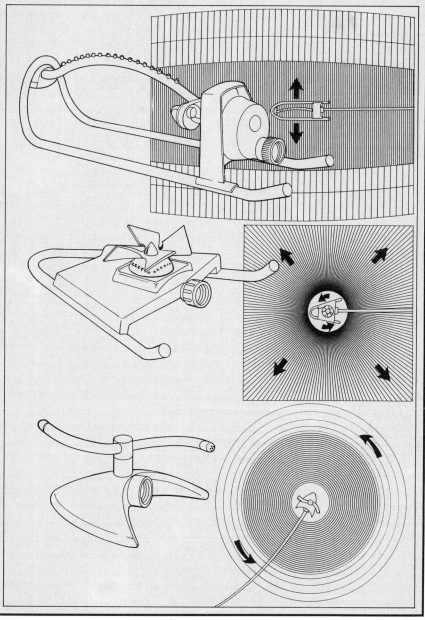

June

Roses

With its long history in cultivation dating back to Persian and Roman times, the rose is now the most popular of all garden plants. Over the years it has been developed until it exists in a large number of shapes and colours with a range of fragrances.

CLASSES OF ROSES

Hybrid teas and floribundas   The hybrid teas have shapely flowers produced more or less continuously from June to October. The floribundas, which flower over the same period, have been developed from the old polyantha rose and were at one time characterised by the production of clusters of smaller, less shapely flowers. These opened at more or less the same time so that the colour effect was better than that of the hybrid teas although the individual flowers were less attractive.

Now, however, the flowers of the floribundas are being bred to look more like those of the hybrid tea, although they are still carried in clusters, with the result that the two groups are no longer as distinct as they were.

Shrub roses   Difficult to define exactly, these are good, well branched plants that need little pruning. The flowers can be either small or large and carried in clusters or in twos or threes but are usually produced more or less continuously from June to September. The shrub roses are ideal for planting under or mixing in with other shrubs and plants.

Old fashioned roses   Similar to the shrub roses in many ways, requiring little pruning and often looking their best when grown as specimens on their own, the old-fashioned roses are made up of many of the old classes. These include the Moss roses with moss-like outgrowth on the buds and young stems, the Bourbon with very shapely flowers, the Cabbage Roses with many-petalled flowers, the Damask roses, Provence roses, Musk roses and many more. Many are highly perfumed but most flower in June and July only. There are a number of modern hybrids.

Miniature roses   Tiny flowers on little bushes growing to not much more than 45 cm (18 in) are the characteristics of this group. They are useful for edging rose beds or growing in containers.

Species roses   These are the wild roses, some of which have been used as parents of the garden

hybrids. Most have single flowers which bloom only once a year and some have very handsome hips which follow the flowering. *Rosa moyesii* and *R. pomifera* are good examples of this. The species roses are best used to provide a background to other roses.

Ramblers and climbers   Ramblers are vigorous climbers which carry quantities of small flowers but only produce them once in early summer. Not many new varieties are being raised as they are gradually being superseded by the repeat-flowering climbers which produce their flowers over a much longer season.

SCENTED ROSES

Scent is an asset to any rose and this is especially the case if it is to be planted near the house where its fragrance can be enjoyed through the open window on a summer's evening.

1 Grandpa Dickson 2 Roseraie de l'Hay
3 Hips of *Rosa rugosa* with *Sedum* Autumn Joy
4 *Rosa canina* Andersonii, a hybrid of the dog rose
5 The climbing rose Albertine

Most of the classes of old-fashioned rose are highly scented and these would be a good choice for such a position. Hybrid teas and floribundas especially noted for their scent are: Alec's Red, crimson; Bonsoir, peach-pink; Duke of Windsor, vermilion; Eden Rose, deep pink; Ernest H. Morse, red; Fragrant Cloud, coral flame; Arthur Bell, yellow; Dearest, salmon pink.

ROSE HEDGES

A rose hedge can be particularly effective especially if a shrub rose which produces colourful hips in the autumn is used. The rose chosen depends on the site and purpose. The *rugosa* roses are excellent for boundary hedges and do well in a cold or difficult position but they do take up a lot of room and you will need to allow 2 m (6 ft) in width for them. Other old-fashioned and shrub roses which are suitable include the

Hybrid Musks and Bourbons and the striped *Rosa* Mundi is particularly effective for a low-growing hedge to 1 m (3 ft) or so. Floribundas which make good hedges include Queen Elizabeth, Masquerade and Chinatown.

The planting of briars such as *canina*, *laxa* and *multiflora*, which are often sold for this purpose, is not recommended.

PLANTING FOR EFFECT

Usually I am of the opinion that plants look better in mixtures but assortments of roses, and in particular the hybrid teas and floribundas, do not look well as all too often their lovely colours can detract from each other. It is far better to plant in blocks of one variety and to organise it so that adjacent blocks blend or provide contrast to each other. In smaller areas where, perhaps only ten or twelve roses at the most are planted, then I would recommend that these are made up of two or three varieties. Some rose colours are especially difficult to blend, the brilliant vermilion orange of a variety such as Orange Sensation is an example and with this I find it is best to use a white such as Iceberg.

If you do plan to grow some of the more brilliant colours, it is advisable to try to see some of the flowers arranged together so that you can get an accurate idea of what their colours will look like when growing together. Although it is not impossible to move roses, they do not like being disturbed and it is better to try to get the planting right in the first place.

Inside

Some form of shading will be needed on the greenhouse or conservatory, especially if gloxinias, begonias, streptocarpus and fuchsias are being grown. Give plenty of air and damp down the floors and staging at least once a day to maintain a moist atmosphere.

Whitefly is a likely and troublesome pest, especially if tomatoes are being grown, and the greenhouse will need fumigating with HCH smoke pellets or cones every 14 days or so against this pest.

Sowing   There is very little of this to be done at the moment with the exception of a number of primulas for spring flowering. Well worthwhile sowing are *Primula denticulata*, *P.* Wanda, *P. rosea* and *P. malacoides*.

Pricking out   The seedlings of cineraria and large-flowered calecolaria may now be ready for pricking out. Shade the young plants from strong sunshine.

Potting   Many plants will be in need of potting on and this should not be neglected. I make sure that any plants which appear to be on the dry side are well watered an hour or so before the potting.

Begonias and gloxinias   Those grown from seed should be potted into their final 5- or 6-in pots using John Innes potting compost No. 2, or a peat-based compost. These will flower from late July to October.

Flowers on the begonias started from tubers may now be in need of a stake. Staking and tying should be done carefully as the stems are rather brittle.

Carnations   Pot on perpetual flowering carnations into 8-in pots and John Innes potting compost No. 1, or a peat-based compost.

Chrysanthemums   Another job to be done now is to pot the indoor flowering chrysanthemums into their final 9-in pots. Pots of this size are expensive these days, and over the last two years I have used black polythene pots and found them very good and much cheaper.

I use John Innes potting compost No. 3 for the final potting and do not fill the pots completely, leaving 5 cm (2 in) at the top for topdressing later

Use a piece of wood to firm the compost in large pots.

on. From now until September these will stand outside, each plant supported by a strong 1.5 m (5 ft) cane.

Spray chrysanthemums at regular intervals with an insecticide to keep down aphids and other pest.

Cyclamen   Young cyclamen plants, resulting from sowings last summer and now in 3- or 3½-in pots, are ready for their final 5- or 6-in pots. I find these do better in a peat-based compost. After potting keep the plants in cool, moist, shady conditions—outdoors in a shaded garden frame would be ideal. Cyclamen seed can be sown in pots or boxes of seed compost and kept in a temperature of 15°C (59°F) until they have germinated.

Cuttings   Pot up the softwood cuttings taken earlier and set out in the garden frame to harden off before planting out.

VEGETABLES

Cucumbers are now growing quickly and need regular attention in the way of stopping, training and feeding. If grown on mounds of compost, these will now need topdressing every other week with about 1 cm (½ in) of John Innes potting compost No. 3 or a peat-based compost. It may be necessary to water twice on warm sunny days.

The cucumbers in the garden frame must also be kept well watered. Pinch out the growing tip when six leaves have formed, and train four of the resulting side shoots to the corners of the frame, stopping each at the second leaf. Place a slate or piece of glass under each cucumber as it develops. As with cucumbers grown in the greenhouse, the male flowers must be removed before they have a chance to fertilise the female ones.

Tomatoes, too, should be growing fast and setting fruit. Take out all side shoots before they have a chance to develop

Shading the greenhouse

In order to keep down the temperature and also to prevent plants from scorching, some form of shading should be used on the greenhouse. The most flexible method is undoubtedly a system of roller blinds which can be raised or lowered easily whenever the need arises. Such blinds may be of fabric or polythene if used inside the house or of wooden lath or split cane if used outside. A cheaper alternative is to paint the glass with a proprietary shading compound or whitewash but, since this must remain in position until washed off, it may well create problems by reducing the light available inside the house during periods of dull weather.

Shading alone will not control the temperature level in summer if adequate ventilation is not available. Greenhouses should always be supplied with ventilators near the ridge and, if possible, in the sides to give a through current of air. Fitting the ventilators with automatic opening devices as shown here (near right) can be a great advantage for the gardener who is away from home during the day.

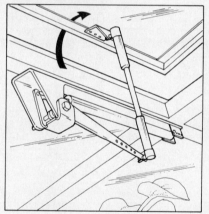

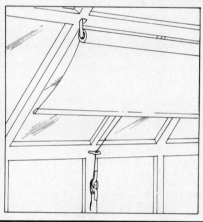

and feed regularly. Those growing in peat bags may need feeding as frequently as three times a week.

Regular and sufficient supplies of water are especially important for tomatoes. Erratic watering often causes blackened areas to develop at the base of the fruits. This condition is known as blossom end rot.

One job which must not be neglected is the regular removal of the side shoots on tomato plants. These grow in the angles between the leaves and main stem.

HOUSE PLANTS

Many of the house plants will benefit from being stood out of doors for the summer months. Choose a sheltered, partially shaded position for them and water regularly.

Those remaining indoors may suffer from the heat and dry atmosphere. Spray the leaves with water each day, or stand the pots in the bath and spray them thoroughly each week. Watch out for attacks of greenfly and whitefly, and spray with one of the insecticides especially prepared for use on house plants.

July

'A swarm of bees
in July
is not worth
a fly'

Now that we are well on into summer it is important to organise
the garden work so that we have time to relax in the garden
and enjoy it. I always find this easier said than done! Although
you may be tempted to do so it is never wise to neglect the weeds;
if left they produce seeds and then you are really in trouble.
'One year's seeds, Seven years weeds' goes another of those
old sayings with so much truth behind it. Weeding in the vegetable
garden is best done with the hoe but elsewhere it is sometimes
possible to take the easier way out and use chemical
weedkillers. One such is paraquat which is economical and effective
if used while the weeds are small. This becomes inactive in
the soil but will kill all leaves and young stems with which it
comes in contact. I find it only necessary to keep the cat
and dog shut up during the period when I am using
the weedkiller and for about half an hour afterwards.

The paths and drives can be treated with what is known as
residual weedkiller and this remains active for several months,
killing the weeds as they emerge. Like other garden chemicals,
weedkillers should always be handled with care and applied
exactly as directed by the makers. It is best to keep one watering
can, clearly labelled, especially for this purpose to prevent
any mishap.

I am often asked about fairy rings on lawns and how to cure
them. Even if the unmistakeable ring of toadstools is absent,
the presence of the fungus is indicated by rings of dark green grass.
The fungus moves through the soil by means of a mycelium
(or spawn) and this has a tendency to seal the surface and prevent
water soaking in. It is mainly through lack of moisture that
the centre of the ring becomes pale brown and looks poor.
The whole area of the ring must be forked to a depth of
8 to 10 cm (3 to 4 in) and a few feet beyond the ring of darker
grass. It should then be watered with a weak solution
of household detergent which acts as a wetting agent and helps
the water soak in. Finally dust thoroughly with calomel dust
and water this in with a solution of detergent. I find this usually
does the trick.

Outside

TREES AND SHRUBS

Pruning Continue to prune shrubs as they finish flowering, cutting out some of the older branches to encourage new growth for flowering next year.

Climbers Train in the growths of climbing plants as they develop otherwise they may get tangled. If *Clematis montana* has finished flowering it can be cut back as required to fill its allotted space.

Roses Cut back the dead or fading flowers to a prominent bud or new shoot. This will stimulate more growth and provide flowers a little later in the summer.

You are likely to see strong young shoots, many of them rich red in colour, growing from the bases of the rose bushes. These shoots differ in appearance from suckers, with which they should not be confused, and they normally grow vigorously and provide good flowers. In the case of rambler roses these new shoots will be the flowering branches for next year and they should be carefully tied into their supports.

It is advisable to spray yet again if there are any signs of mildew.

FLOWERS

There is still time to sow the spring-flowering biennials early in the month. Some of those sown last month should now have reached a reasonable size and can be planted: I generally use part of the vegetable garden for this. Sprinkle some general garden fertiliser over the surface and lightly fork the soil over, firm by treading and then rake it down fine and even. I prefer to make shallow drills, and to plant the seedlings 23 cm (9 in) apart along the drills. This makes watering much easier.

The seedlings of both polyanthus and primroses sown earlier in the year in the greenhouse are now ready for planting out in the way just described. They will appreciate a partially shaded spot.

General care Now that sweet peas are flowering, regular removal of side shoots and the tying of the main shoots to supports are necessary. Frequent watering and feeding will help to keep the plants producing strong stems.

Those sweet peas which are not being trained should have the flowers cut regularly. Failing this, any fading flowers should be removed to prevent the formation of seed pods.

As the flower spikes on both lupins and delphiniums fade, so they should be cut off.

Many of the taller growing hardy annuals now need some form of support to prevent them from being dashed down by rain and wind. A good means of support is achieved by pushing twiggy branches or pea sticks into the soil between and around the plants. Take off all fading flowers.

Water frequently and feed tubs and other containers and hanging baskets.

Feed also outdoors chrysanthemums and dahlias. Scatter a general fertiliser around the plants, keeping it away from the stems, and stir it into the surface with a hoe.

Water well if dry.

Stake the taller varieties of dahlias securely as the stems are brittle. Towards the end of the month it may be necessary to thin out the dahlia shoots if the plants look overcrowded.

Border carnations can be easily increased by layering.

Layering carnations *Above* Choose a suitable side shoot and make a cut into the stem. *Below* Anchor the cut portion into a handful of sand placed on the soil.

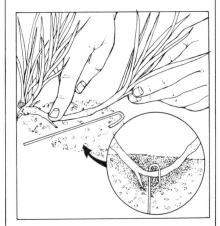

The rock garden Take cuttings of all the early flowering plants. Pieces pulled off and inserted in sand and peat in a frame or a box, with a sheet of glass or polythene over the top, will root well.

THE LAWN

At this time whenever there are a few days of dry sunny weather, I put the sprinklers on the lawn in an attempt to keep it looking green and lush.

Those areas where the grass was left uncut until last month because the daffodil leaves had not properly died down, may be looking a little brown and bare. Fork them over, apply a dressing of fertiliser and water well.

VEGETABLES

Sowing We should now be digging the early potatoes and should have cleared the early peas and autumn sown broad beans. The spaces in the vegetable plot can be used for further sowings of stump-rooted carrots, globe beetroot, lettuce, radish, Chinese cabbage, and leaf beet. Before sowing, fork the soil and sprinkle a general fertiliser over the surface (a handful to the sq m or yd), tread to make the soil firm and rake it finely. Watering along the drills hastens germination.

Ridge cucumbers Pinch the tip out of the stem when six leaves have formed and train the resulting side shoots around the plant. Do not remove the male flowers, unlike other kinds of cucumber these require pollination.

Watering and feeding The onions should be swelling now and it is worth giving them one more feed with nitrate of soda lightly hoed into the soil around the bulbs. To feed too late in the summer tends to make them form thick necks and they will not ripen off properly.

Water well when the weather is dry paying particular attention to celery, leeks, marrows, courgettes, cucumbers, beans and tomatoes. Begin feeding the outdoor tomatoes with liquid tomato fertiliser

Layering strawberries

This is a good time to increase strawberries. Select runners from the healthiest plants, taking not more than six from each plant. Press the plantlet nearest to the plant on each runner into a $3\frac{1}{2}$-in pot of potting compost using a hairpin-shaped piece of wire to keep the runner in place. Cut off the extension runners. Sink the pots into the soil around the plants.

and feed the marrows, courgettes and ridge cucumbers with liquid fertiliser.

Sprinkle a general fertiliser along the runner bean rows and water in. Spray the plants overhead with water during the day to assist the setting of the flowers, and remember: a lack of moisture at the roots is one of the main causes of bud drop.

Pest control Take precautions against cabbage root fly, onion fly and carrot fly by dusting an insecticidal dust around the stems of all members of the brassica family and along rows of carrots and onions.

Look for, and squash, any caterpillars of the cabbage white butterfly.

FRUIT

As strawberries finish fruiting, spray them over with

insecticide to prevent aphids transmitting virus disease, clear away the straw or matting and clean up the beds.

Spray raspberries, blackberries and loganberries with derris to prevent attack by the grubs of the raspberry beetle. Always spray in the evening so that the bees are unharmed.

Any branches on the plum trees which show signs of silver leaf disease should be cut out and burned. This disease causes a metallic silvering of the leaf, and should not be confused with mildew which produces a powdery white covering to the leaves.

If apples have set a lot of fruit, they may require thinning out. I always take out the king fruit, which is the one in the centre of each cluster.

July

Plants of the Month

This is the month when the bedding plants and annuals will be at their best providing bright continuous colour to offset the shrubs and border plants. It is also the time when some of the most spectacular and popular of the hardy plants will be flowering.

SHRUBS and CLIMBERS

Carpenteria   For a sheltered corner and light soil, the evergreen *C. californica* is a good choice. It has large waxy, white fragrant flowers. Prune in spring, cutting out some of the older stems to the base.

Clematis   In flower now are many of the hybrids with spectacular large flowers in a wide range of colours. These succeed best on a rather limy soil. Position them so that the roots are shaded but the stems are in full sun. Prune in February or March, cutting out dead and damaged growth and shortening the remaining shoots a little.

Hydrangea   Good for sun or partial shade. The colours are affected by the soil: in an acid soil the pink or red varieties become blue or purple whilst the reverse happens on an alkaline soil. It is possible to 'blue' some varieties with chemical treatment. There is a climbing hydrangea—*petiolaris*—which has flat clusters of white flowers and may grow to 15 m (50 ft).

Hypericum (St. John's Wort)   Very good ground cover for a reasonable soil and sun or partial shade. Deciduous and evergreen kinds, all with large yellow flowers. *Hypericum calycinum* and *H. moserianum* can be pruned back almost to ground level in spring. Most kinds are under 60 cm (2 ft).

Lavender   Fragrant evergreen shrubs suitable for well drained soils and a sunny position. Especially good on chalky soils. Trim over with the shears as soon as the flowers fade.

Phlomis (Jerusalem Sage)   Fine evergreen shrub with yellow flowers and growing to 1 m (3 ft) high. It needs warmth, sun and good drainage. Trim back in spring to keep it from becoming straggly.

Spiraea   Deciduous shrubs for any soil and open place. A very good variety is *Spiraea japonica* Anthony Waterer with pink flowers and some leaves which show cream variegation; it is better for being hard pruned in March.

FLOWERING PLANTS

Ageratum   Half-hardy annual, 15 to 45 cm (6 to 18 in) tall, producing fluffy flowers in white or shades of blue or purple throughout most of the summer.

Althaea (Hollyhock)   This perennial is often grown as a biennial, although in well drained soil and a sunny position it may survive for several years. Growing up to 2·5 m (8 ft) tall with familiar heads of flowers, which are double in some varieties.

Calendula (Marigold)   Well-known hardy annual growing to 60 cm (2 ft) high with yellow or orange daisy flowers. Remove flowers as soon as they fade to prevent masses of self-sown seedlings.

Delphinium   Medium to tall perennial plants, some growing up to 2 m (6 ft) high. They succeed best in a sunny place and rich well drained soil. The heavy flower spikes are in all shades of blue, mauve, white, pink and red. There are two main groups, the tall Elatum varieties and the shorter Belladonna varieties.

Dianthus (Pinks)   These perennial plants do best in an open sunny place, are not particular about soil and grow up to 38 cm (15 in). The flowers are mostly in shades of pink and crimson, also white, and some are sweetly scented. The Allwoodii strain have the longest flowering season extending sometimes into September.

1 A colourful mixed planting of lavender, variety Hidcote, and the yellow *Hypericum* Rowallane
2 The lovely pink, *Dianthus* Doris
3 Water lilies, Nymphaea
4 Gloxinia

Eschscholzia (Californian Poppy)   Hardy annual growing to 30 cm (12 in) with poppy-like flowers ranging in colour from white to orange, yellow, pink and red. Best in an open sunny place and rather dry soil.

Lathyrus (Sweet Pea)   Lovely annual with fragrant flowers in a wide range of delicate colours. To see them at their best, plant in an open sunny place on soil which has been well dug and well manured.

Nymphaea (Water Lily)   The many varieties of this lovely aquatic plant need to be planted in baskets filled with good soil and placed on the bottom of the pool, in at least 30 cm (12 in) of water. The flowers are produced from July to September in white, yellow and pink to crimson. Best left undisturbed until they become over-crowded.

Petunia   Half-hardy annual growing to about 45 cm (18 in) high with showy funnel-shaped flowers in most colours, except yellow and orange, produced through the summer. Best in a sunny warm position. Many varieties available, some with very large flowers.

Phlox   Easily grown in sun or shade and producing fragrant flowers in white or shades of pink, mauve and red from now until September. Height 60 cm to 1·25 m (2 to 4 ft).

Tropaeolum (Nasturtium)   Easily grown hardy annual which is not too fussy about soil or position. There are both dwarf and climbing forms with brightly coloured yellow, orange and red flowers.

VEGETABLES IN THE GARDEN

Beetroot, broad beans, French beans, runner beans, cabbage, carrots, cauliflower, leaf beet, lettuce, marrow, onions, peas, early potatoes, radish, spinach, turnips.

FRUIT IN THE GARDEN

Cherries, black, red and white currants, goose-berries, loganberries, raspberries and strawberries.

INSIDE

Begonia   The tuberous-rooted begonias have large, showy flowers in white, pink, red and shades of yellow and orange. Keep well shaded in summer.

Gloxinia   Now more correctly called sinningia, these very showy plants carry their large velvety trumpet-shaped flowers in purple, red, pink and white from July to September. Water well and shade from bright sunshine.

VEGETABLES IN THE GREENHOUSE

Cucumbers, tomatoes.

Inside

Plants in the greenhouse and conservatory will need copious watering and shading from bright sun.

General care Watering is one of the most important tasks this month, and with the holiday season about to start, this may be a problem. There are various methods of automatic watering which work well for pot plants, but if you are growing tomatoes or cucumbers, you have really got to get someone to tend them for you.

Ventilation can be given freely and it is now that the value of automatic ventilators can be appreciated. These work on a fluid which expands as the temperature rises, opening the ventilator, and contracts as the temperature falls, closing the ventilators.

All the pot plants should now be fed regularly to help build up stronger plants and keep the flowering period going until later in the summer. I always ensure that no plant is given liquid fertiliser when the compost in the pot is dry; the plants are given water first and then fertiliser. To feed plants such as this when the compost is dry can cause scorching of the roots and gives a severe check.

Begonias and gloxinias Gloxinias grown from seed sown earlier in the year and now in 5-in pots should be beginning to produce their flowers. Feeding these weekly will not only help to keep the plants flowering, but will help to build up reasonable tubers.

This also applies to the large double flowered begonias.

Carnations Stop the side shoots at four pairs of leaves. Stand plants outside in a shaded frame if possible.

Chrysanthemums Tie in the new shoots as they appear and stop all plants for the second time. Water and feed regularly.

Cinerarias Pot on seedlings into 3½-in pots.

Cyclamen The young plants which were potted into 5-in pots in June should be growing well, but some may be producing flower buds. These buds should be pulled off as they appear in order to build up good strong leafy plants.

This is the time to start into growth the old corms which have been kept from last winter. Water them lightly and, as new leaves appear, repot the plants into fresh compost. Keep the corms slightly above the surface of the compost.

Sowing Sow large-flowered pansies for planting out in the autumn, and also Brompton stocks.

Cuttings Many shrubs can be increased by half-ripe cuttings. These are taken from

shoots where the wood is beginning to get hard at the base. Pull the shoot with a heel of older wood attached and trim this neatly with a knife. Dip the end in hormone rooting powder and then insert in sandy soil in pots or boxes. Place these in a propagating frame or a large polythene bag and shade from strong sun.

The garden pinks can be increased by cuttings, or 'pipings' as they are called. Simply pull out a non-flowering shoot at a joint.

Pelargoniums The regal pelargoniums are better stood out of doors for the next few weeks. The plants should now have finished flowering and it is a convenient time to take cuttings. Make these from firm, non-flowering growth, 8 to 13 cm (3 to 5 in) long. Trim the base cleanly below the leaf joint, remove the lower leaves and dip the end in hormone rooting powder. Insert the cuttings in pots of peat and sand, water well and keep shaded.

Pot up the rooted cuttings of

Half-ripe cuttings with a 'heel'.

Trim and insert in a pot of compost.

Watering in greenhouse and home

If you are unable to attend regularly to the watering of greenhouse plants at this time of year then it is worth-while to install a system of automatic watering. One of the simplest ways of doing this is by using capillary matting contained in large trays and fed with water from a reservoir—usually either a tank with a ball valve or a large upturned bottle. The base of each pot must be firmly placed on the matting so that the compost is in contact with the matting through the drainage holes and can draw water from it.

House plants The watering of house plants during holiday time can present quite a problem unless there is a neighbour who will come in and take care of it for you. Plants can survive for quite long periods if they are well watered and then placed in a sink or bath and packed around with damp newspaper. Alternatively, a wick of absorbent tape anchored in the compost and led up into a container of water will do the trick. The container of water must be placed above the plant.

geraniums (correctly called zonal pelargoniums).

Primulas Pot the seedlings of *P. obconica*, *P. sinensis* and *P. malacoides* singly into 3½-in pots for flowering in the greenhouse or conservatory early next year.

Vegetables The cucumbers in the greenhouse should now be producing well. I often hear people say that their cucumbers are very bitter. To be at their best they must grow quickly— those that are slow to grow and develop will be bitter.

A cucumber plant needs warmth, plenty of water on sunny days and feeding with a liquid fertiliser once a week. I feed the cucumbers with liquid tomato fertiliser. Another important point is to pinch the tips from every side shoot at the second leaf.

If it has not been done already, put a little light shading on the glass over where the tomatoes are growing, because on warm sunny days there is a tendency for the sun to cause greenback on those

fruits which are exposed to full sunshine.

The tomato plants should now have reached their maximum height—that is to the roof of the greenhouse—so the top of each one is pinched out one leaf above the highest truss. Remove some of the lower leaves to let light and air get to the fruit.

HOUSE PLANTS

Continue to treat the plants as outlined in June. Feed every ten days or so with a liquid fertiliser.

August

'Dry August and warm
Doth harvest no harm'

Now that the greenery has lost its early summer freshness,
it is more important than ever to keep everything in the garden
tidy. Otherwise it is all too easy for plants to take on a jaded air.
So do continue to pay attention to the weeding, remove all the faded
and dead flowers and cut away any dead leaves.

This month, too, you should turn your attention to hedge clipping,
some, such as the privet, need trimming more than once a year,
but for the majority a once-a-year tidy up is sufficient. And this
should be done no later than August to give the shrubs a chance
to make new growth before the winter. When using shears
hold the blades flat against the hedge as you stand sideways onto it.
In this way you can get a line of sight along the blades and see
more clearly what needs to be removed. The large-leaved
evergreens, such as laurel, should always be trimmed with
secateurs. If hedging shears are used they will cut indiscriminately
through the leaves and you will be left with many unsightly
brown edges. Never cut the bottom of a hedge narrower than the
top and if you live in an area where falls of snow are common in
winter then trim the top to a point to prevent the snow from lying
and damaging the hedge with its weight.

When dealing with young hedges, especially those of beech,
hornbeam, *Cupressocyparis leylandii*, *Chamaecyparis lawsoniana*
and thujas such as *plicata*, it is advisable to allow them to
reach the required height before taking out the tops. In the
meantime just trim the ends of the branches to encourage them to
thicken up.

The more informal kinds of flowering hedges which include those
of berberis, pyracantha, escallonia and rose, should never be
trimmed too hard or they will produce few flowers. It is best just
to go over them occasionally with secateurs to remove any long or
straggly growths.

78

CHECK LIST

Clip hedges
Prune rambler roses
Disbud dahlias and
    chrysanthemums
Treat lawn for weeds
Summer prune apples
Cut back blackcurrants
    and raspberries
Sow onions
Earth up celery
Order bulbs

Outside

TREES AND SHRUBS

Pruning   Clip lavender bushes over as soon as they finish flowering, this prevents them becoming bare at the base.

Roses   Prune ramblers as they finish flowering. Cut out to ground level those growths which have just carried flowers and tie in the new stems made this year. This job is made easier if you untie all the stems and spread them out on the ground before you start pruning.

   Continue to check roses for the presence of suckers and cut or pull these off from the point of origin on the rootstock.

   If mildew is showing on the roses then continue to spray every two weeks or so.

FLOWERS

Planting   The beginning of the month is the latest time to plant colchicums (autumn-flowering crocuses) and hardy spring-flowering cyclamen. Cyclamen do best when planted as pot-grown plants rather than dry tubers.

   Most lilies are planted in November except for the Madonna lily, *Lilium candidum*, which should be planted now. Cover the bulbs with an inch of soil.

   Continue to plant out spring-flowering seedlings (page 72). It is important to do this early so that the seedlings make good sturdy plants before winter sets in.

   The winter-flowering pansies should also be planted out in a similar manner as soon as they are large enough to handle.

   If weather remains dry for a few days, regular watering will be necessary until it is obvious

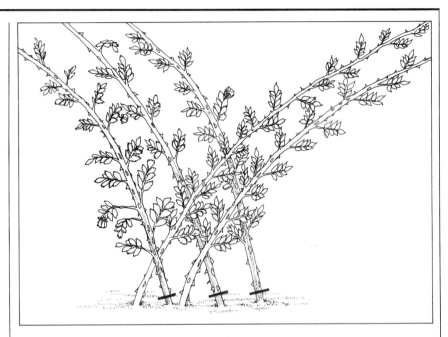

Cut out the old flowering stems of rambler roses at ground level and tie in the strong young shoots.

the plants are well established.

   Cuttings of pinks taken last month, and the layers of the border carnations, should be rooted and ready for planting out towards the end of August or in early September.

Chrysanthemums   Unless grown for spray flowers, disbud the chrysanthemums to leave one flower bud on each stem, and remove all side shoots.

Dahlias   With the exception of the pompons and small flowered types, dahlias should also be disbudded to leave one flower bud to each stem.

   Earwigs can be quite a pest on dahlias, eating the buds and damaging the petals. Flower pots filled with hay and inverted on canes among the plants make effective traps.

Remove chrysanthemum side shoots.

Remove all but the central bud.

Inspect them each day and dispose of any insects.

The rock garden Cuttings of the rock plants taken earlier can be planted out as soon as they are rooted. Alternatively, they can be kept in pots in a frame until spring.

THE LAWN

Continue to water the grass in periods of dry weather. I often notice patches of white clover and yarrow on my lawn at this time of year, so I like to apply a lawn fertiliser with an added selective weedkiller.

VEGETABLES

Many vegetables are now ready for picking and the secret is to harvest them while they are young and tender. At this stage they are ideal for freezing.

Sowing As crops are harvested and the plants cleared the ground should be filled again with sowings of lettuce, spinach and turnips, or planted up with cabbages and other winter greens.

Spring cabbage can be sown early in August in the North of the country and later in the month in the South.

From the middle of the month I like to sow onions. Some of these will be Japanese varieties which have the advantage of maturing early in the summer, so that the bulbs have a chance to get well ripened and thus keep well. Other varieties suitable for this sowing are Autumn Queen and Ailsa Craig. For producing spring onions for pulling green there are few varieties better than White Lisbon. Prepare the soil as previously described (page 36) and sow the seeds thinly along drills.

General care Towards the middle of the month, turn the tops over on the spring-sown onions. This helps to check the growth and hastens ripening.

To keep onions through the winter they must be well ripened before bad weather sets in.

Continue to water and feed runner beans or, better still, water with liquid fertiliser.

Feed Brussels sprouts and other winter greens with general fertiliser.

Begin to earth up the celery. Put bands of newspaper— 8 to 10 cm (3 to 4 in) in width— around the plants before drawing up the soil. This helps to keep the stems cleaner and to prevent slug damage. Never bring the earth up above the growing points or you will encourage heart rot.

The maincrop potatoes can be lifted from this month onwards.

Gather herbs, bind in bunches, wash and hang up to dry.

Pest control Spray brassica plants to control caterpillars and to keep cabbage whitefly and grey aphids in check. Spray the later sown broad beans to prevent blackfly damage.

Pruning hedges

Unless it is kept unclipped, a hedge needs trimming at least once a year to prevent the base from becoming bare and the top straggly. When cutting the sides with shears, keep the blades flat to the face of the hedge. Then, standing on a stool or ladder if necessary so that you can look down on the hedge, cut the top: place a line at the height required and make the first cut along the length of line with the shears turned over (see below). Then cut along the rest of the top with the shears the right way up taking the line first cut as a guide.

Electric hedge trimmers make the whole job easier. Keep them oiled regularly as sap removes the oil and impairs the efficiency of the blades. When using the trimmer keep the flex over the shoulder and well away from the blades. Tilt the blades slightly inwards towards the hedge and cup upwards in smooth strokes.

Conifer hedges should be allowed to reach the required height before the tops of the plants are taken off. To do this, use a line to mark the height and cut along this.

August

Plants of the Month

This can be a rather inbetween month in the garden, with many of the early and midsummer flowers going over, and the late flowers still to come. There should be a second crop of roses to give colour, and plants such as lavatera and phlox which flower generously over quite a long period, also the large-flower hybrid clematis.

SHRUBS

Buddleia (Butterfly Bush)   Easily grown deciduous shrubs which succeed well on chalk. One of the most popular is *Buddleia davidii* with pale lavender flowers. There are varieties with white or purple flowers. All will reach a height of between 2 and 3·5 m (6 and 12 ft) and can be cut back hard in March if required.

Calluna (Heather)   Small evergreen shrubs growing to 60 cm (2 ft) and thriving in an acid peaty soil, and sunny or lightly shaded position. Many varieties with flowers ranging from white to crimson. Cut back lightly in the spring.

Ceanothus (Californian Lilac)   The deciduous varieties of ceanothus flower in late summer and enjoy a well-drained soil and sheltered position. Some grow to about 2 m (6 ft), others are shorter. Flowers in blue, violet, or pink according to variety; cut hard back in March.

Hebe (Veronica)   Evergreen shrubs, some of which are inclined to be tender, which produce spikes of flowers in white, pink, red, purple or blue from July to October. They like sun but are not particular about soil, and grow from 30 cm to 1.25 m (4 ft) or so. Cut back in spring if over-grown. Some of the most attractive are Carl Teschner, violet; Midsummer Beauty, white tinged with lavender and Great Orme, pink.

Hibiscus   For a warm sunny position, the deciduous *Hibiscus syriacus* has much to recommend it as a late-flowering shrub. It may reach 3 m (10 ft) tall and carries hollyhock-like flowers, some double, in white, pink, mauve or blue. Cut out weak or damaged wood in spring.

FLOWERING PLANTS

Antirrhinum (Snapdragon)   Half-hardy perennial usually grown as an half-hardy annual and succeeding best in a well drained soil and a sunny open place. There are dwarf, medium and tall varieties from 15 cm to 1 m (6 in to 3 ft), with flowers in a wide colour range. As well as

the familiar pouched flowers, there are varieties with double flowers.

Chrysanthemum (Shasta Daisy)   Easily grown perennials for an open position and reasonable soil. The large white daisies, which are derived from *Chrysanthemum maximum*, are as useful for cutting as providing garden colour. To about 75 cm (2½ ft) tall.

Cosmos (Cosmea)   Half-hardy and hardy annuals with daisy flowers in pink, crimson, white and yellow with delicate fern-like foliage which grow best in an open and sunny position. Ranging in height from 45 cm to 1·25 m (1½ to 4 ft).

Dimorphotheca (Star of the Veldt)   Slightly tender annual for a sunny position with well-drained soil, which grows to about 38 cm (15 in) and produces daisy flowers in white, yellow, apricot or orange. Can be sown outdoors in April or early May.

Erigeron   Mostly easily grown perennial plants for any soil and an open position. Growing to between 30 and 60 cm (1 and 2 ft) high with daisy flowers in blue, mauve, pink, rose and orange. *Erigeron mucronatus* is a small species which grows well on a sunny wall.

82

1 Cosmos
2 Star of the Veldt, *Dimorphotheca aurantiaca*
3 Helenium
4 *Gladiolus* Miss America
5 A magnificent display of *Lilium regale* with delphiniums, golden rod and catmint

probably need individual staking. Lift the corms after flowering and dry off. Plant in April.

Lilium (Lily) Many of the spectacular species and hybrid lilies will be in flower this month. Ranging in height from 60 cm to 2 m (2 to 7 ft) they thrive in partial shade and deep soils containing plenty of peat or leafmould. One of the most brilliant is the Tiger lily, *Lilium tigrinum*.

VEGETABLES IN THE GARDEN

Broad beans, French beans, runner beans, beetroot, cabbage, carrots, cauliflower, celery, ridge cucumbers, leaf beet, lettuce, marrows, onions, peas, potatoes (maincrop) radish, spinach, sweet corn, tomatoes, turnips.

FRUIT IN THE GARDEN

Apples, blackberries, cherries, black, red and white currants, gooseberries, loganberries, pears, plums.

INSIDE

Browallia An annual which makes a pretty pot plant with its large blue or white flowers produced from July to September or in the autumn depending on the sowing time: February or March in the former case, May or June for later flowering.

Coleus Richly coloured foliage plants which are easily raised from seed sown in early spring, or cuttings rooted in a propagator in spring or summer.

VEGETABLES IN THE GREENHOUSE

Cucumbers, tomatoes.

Helenium Perennial with daisy flowers in yellow or brownish-red for most soils and an open position. Good varieties, which vary in height between 1 and 2 m (3 and 6 ft), include Crimson Beauty, brownish-red; Moerheim Beauty, bronze-red and Golden Youth.

Lavatera (Tree Mallow) In a light soil and sheltered position, *Lavatera olbia* makes a many-branched bush growing to about 2 m (7 ft) tall which carries quantities of pink flowers in late summer. The growth may be damaged by frost in winter and any such damaged stems should be cut back in spring.

Verbascum (Mullein) The long narrow flower spikes vary in height from 60 cm to 2 m (2 to 6 ft) according to variety, and colours range from white through yellow and bronze to pink and purple. All thrive in well drained even poor sandy soils and a sunny position.

BULBS

Gladiolus For a sunny position and rich well drained soil the gladioli make a brilliant show with their heavy flower spikes in all colours. The taller varieties, which may grow to 1·25 m (4 ft), will

FRUIT

Pruning The summer-fruiting raspberries have now finished cropping, so now is the time to cut out all the canes which have just fruited. Loosely tie in the young canes, thinning these to leave one every 23 cm (9 in). Feed with a general garden fertiliser sprinkled along each side of the row.

Blackcurrants can also be pruned now, as many as possible of the old fruiting branches being cut out to encourage young shoots to grow. These are the ones that will produce the crop next year. Sprinkle 110 g (4 oz) of fertiliser

Raspberry canes which have just fruited are cut out at ground level and the new canes tied in.

on the soil around each plant to encourage new growth.

I like to do the summer pruning of trained trees such as cordons and espaliers during the second week of August. Some of the stronger growths are left unpruned, and these I tie down below the horizontal. These will increase the fruiting area and usually carry a really good crop. All the remaining young branches are cut back to 4 or 5 leaves from the point where growth commenced, and the extension branches (the young branch at the tip of each cordon and at each main branch of an espalier-trained tree) cut back to about half their length.

Strawberries Remove any runners formed on existing strawberries, and plant out the young plants as soon as possible this month. Space them 60 cm (2 ft) apart with 75 cm (2½ ft) between the rows.

Trained apples and pears should be summer pruned by cutting side shoots back to 4 or 5 leaves from the base.

Left Blackcurrants produce their best fruit on young wood and so the branches which have just borne fruit should be cut out. The young growth is retained.

Inside

Bulbs should be ordered now for Christmas and winter flowering in pots and bowls. Specially treated bulbs must be used if flowers are wanted in time for Christmas. Some of the easiest to have in flower early are Roman hyacinths and Paper White and Grand Soleil d'Or narcissi.

Cuttings Continue to take half-ripe cuttings of shrubs as described last month.

Some of the shrub cuttings put in early last month should now have rooted and can be potted separately into 3½-in pots. Although some kinds take longer to form their roots than others, forsythia, spiraea, hebe, ribes and ceanothus will probably be among the first. After potting, the cuttings need watering and shading from the sun until they get established.

Seedlings Prick out Brompton stocks as soon as they are large enough to handle. The young seedlings can then be planted out in the garden.

Sowing Schizanthus, salpiglossis and East Lothian and Beauty of Nice stocks should all be sown now to provide flowering plants for the greenhouse and conservatory next spring.

There is still time to sow cyclamen seed. These need from 15 to 18 months from sowing to make good flowering plants. When sowing make sure that the seed is covered by at least 6 mm (¼ in) of compost.

Calceolarias and cinerarias Pot on the seedlings of caleolarias into 3½-in pots.

Pot on cinerarias into 6-in pots.

Chrysanthemums At the end of last month these should have been stopped for the last time. Some people will say this is far too late for stopping chrysanthemums, but I find that this late stopping produces the flowers when they are most needed—over the Christmas period.

If roots appear on the surface of the compost, they are ready for topdressing with John Innes potting compost No. 3. Before putting on the topdressing each plant should be given a small pinch of rose fertiliser because it has the extra potash and extra magnesium needed for the production of good flowers. Any plants which show signs of dryness in the compost must be watered thoroughly before the topdressing is put on.

Remove all flower buds and side shoots to leave one flower on each stem.

Cyclamen Water old corms more freely. Prick out earlier sown seed.

Geraniums Although more correctly called zonal pelargoniums, these plants are usually known as geraniums. They make marvellous flowering plants for frost-free greenhouses and conservatories in March and April of the following year. Cuttings can be taken now as previously described (page 32), and rooted in pots of sandy compost or even in a partially shaded border out of doors.

Once rooted, they should be potted up into 3½ in pots and kept in a temperature of 7 to 13°C (45 to 55°F) during the winter.

Primulas Pot on the young plants of *P. obconica*, *P. sinensis* into their final 5-in pots.

Cucumbers Continue to topdress the planting mounds with John Innes potting compost No. 3 or a peat-based compost as the white roots show above the surface.

It is essential to cut all cucumbers as soon as they are ready, otherwise the young cucumbers which are still growing will be brought to a standstill and will turn yellow at the ends.

Tomatoes Continue to water frequently and feed regularly. Remove some of the leaves from the lower part of the plants to allow the sun to ripen the fruits. I like to do this by cutting the leaves in half.

HOUSE PLANTS

Keep a watch for pests. Continue to water and feed regularly.

Most of the plants can still be readily increased from cuttings. These should be inserted in pots of peat and sand and placed in a propagating frame or inside a large polythene bag.

Cuttings of many of the house plants taken now will root easily.

September

'September blows soft
Till the fruit's
in the loft'

This month sees the beginning of the main harvesting season. It is also the last month of the year which is likely to be free from frost, and towards the very end of the month we must be prepared for this eventuality if the evening has a chilly nip to the air. Frosty nights mean that all the half-hardy perennial plants such as the geraniums and fuchsias, which have been in the garden and in tubs on the patio, must be rehoused if they are to survive the winter.

Apart from the picking and preserving of fruit and harvesting of vegetables, we should be considering how the garden will look in the spring, and begin the planting of bulbs and other spring-flowering plants. The term 'bulb' is often used by gardeners to cover all the plants which grow from some form of swollen underground storage organ which in fact can be either a tuber, rhizome, corm or a true bulb. Crocuses, daffodils and tulips are among the most popular 'bulbs' but there are others which can be counted on to give a good display such as the snowdrops (galanthus), snowflakes (leucojum), grape hyacinths (muscari) winter aconite (eranthis), anemones and iris.

A useful tip when planting bulbs in soil inclined to be heavy, is to drop a small handful of sand into each hole. This helps to prevent water accumulating underneath the bulb and causing it to decay. When planting a quantity of bulbs make all the holes first, set the bulbs in place and then fill the holes in one operation using a rake. To plant for naturalising in grass, I always scatter a handful of bulbs over the grass and plant them where they rest. To make this job easier there is a useful tool called a bulb planter which removes a plug of soil and turf and allows the bulbs to be dropped in place. The plug can be replaced and firmed gently over the bulb.

CHECK LIST
Tidy up
Make compost heap
Plant bulbs
Make lawn from seed
Plant conifers
Harvest onions
Pick apples and pears
Bring in house plants
Pot up bulbs

September

Outside

There is likely to be a lot of tidying up needed now in the garden, and it is well worthwhile collecting together all the various bits of waste from the vegetable garden (stems of broad beans, peas, potato tops etc), the weeds which have probably grown so well over the past few weeks, and the tops cut from the hardy border plants for use on the compost heap. When making this heap sprinkle a compost accelerator and a covering of soil over each 23 cm (9 in) layer of waste.

TREES AND SHRUBS

Now is the time to start planting conifers and other evergreens.

There is little pruning to be done but the climbers need some care. Tie in shoots and cut back if they are taking up too much space.

Roses   Continue to take off the fading flowers, cutting each back to a prominent bud or shoot. This will encourage late flowers which may go into November.

FLOWERS

Towards the end of the month, clear away all the annuals and other bedding plants and prepare the ground for replanting with the spring flowering plants.

Lift gladiolus plants whole, tie in bunches and hang in a shed to dry.

It is a good idea to protect any remaining blooms on the outdoor chrysanthemums by tying a paper bag supported on a wire frame over the head of each.

Bulb planting   September is the beginning of the main bulb planting time, although I like to leave those bulbs which are to be naturalised in grass until next month, because the grass is usually very hard just now. For planting now are anemones, daffodils and other narcissi, scillas and muscari.

All bulbs benefit from a sprinkling of bonemeal worked into the soil around the planting hole. Plant as described on page 86, covering each bulb with approximately twice its own depth of soil.

THE LAWN

Mowing has to be left later in the day now because of the heavy morning dews.

This is the ideal time of year to sow a new lawn, as it gives the grass time to get established before the colder weather sets in.

VEGETABLES

Harvesting   Onions should be lifted early in the month and put in the greenhouse or garden frame where they can be given protection from rain whilst ripening off. Unless thoroughly ripe, they will not store well. Once ripe they can be stored in a dry airy shed, hung either on ropes or in net bags.

Gather French and runner beans regularly, and water if necessary.

Gather the sweet corn before the cobs become too yellow and mealy.

Lift and store carrots and beetroot. I always do this by laying them between layers of sand in boxes, and keeping them in the garden shed. When lifting beetroot, handle it carefully, because if the skin is punctured it will bleed. Similarly remove the leaves with care.

General care   Feed the leeks again with a general garden fertiliser, applying this at the rate of 55 g (2 oz) to the metre or yard row.

Celery is ready for another earthing up, and before drawing the soil up around the sticks, wrap another 10 cm (4 in) band of folded newspaper around each plant to keep the celery cleaner and prevent a lot of slug damage.

Early in the month remove some leaves from the outdoor tomatoes to encourage the fruit to ripen. At the end of the month cut the plants down, put any mature fruit in layers in boxes indoors to finish ripening, and use the small green fruit for chutney.

Pest control   Spray Brussels sprouts again to protect them from caterpillar attack and from the cabbage whitefly. Whilst mixing up the insecticide, make enough to spray other winter crops such as the Savoy and winter cabbage, sprouting broccoli and winter and spring cauliflowers.

Sowing   There is still time to sow the various onion varieties mentioned last month.

Winter lettuce such as Arctic or Imperial can also be sown.

Planting   Prepare the ground where the onions have been for planting the spring cabbage.

FRUIT

Picking   Don't be in too much of a hurry to pick apples. To gather these before they are

Planting bulbs

This is the main bulb planting season and the majority of planting can be done with a trowel. The chart shown here gives an indication of the various depths needed for the different types. The letters given beside the name of each bulb refer to the planting depths in the chart.

Anemone A–B
Chionodoxa B
Colchicum E
Crocus A–B
Eranthis A
Erythronium B
Galanthus A–B
Gladiolus D
Gladiolus species B–C
Hyacinth C
Iris A
Lilies B–F
Muscari B
Narcissus C–E
Narcissus, miniatures A–B
Scilla A–B
Tulip C–D

Unless September is fairly wet, it may be easier to leave naturalising bulbs in grass until next month. The best way to do this is to scatter them in handfuls and then plant them where they

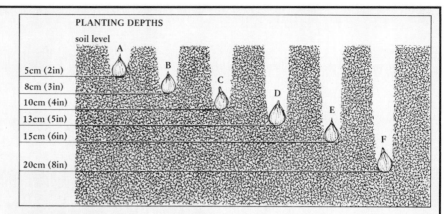

PLANTING DEPTHS
soil level

fall using a special bulb planting tool (right) which removes a plug of soil and turf. The bulbs are placed in the holes and the plugs replaced and gently firmed.

mature will result in bad keeping and shrivelling in store. Varieties likely to be ready will be Beauty of Bath, Worcester Pearmain, Discovery, and some of the early pears. Do not pick the fruit until it parts readily from the tree, and when picking lift the fruit from underneath, levering it gently sideways.

Pest control   Now is the time to put grease bands on fruit trees. This is a simple device which prevents the winter moths crawling up the trees to lay their eggs. The bands and banding compounds are available at garden stores.

I like to spray the blackcurrants, strawberries and raspberries once again this month with systemic insecticide to take care of any late attacks of greenfly. Autumn-fruiting raspberries should not, of course, be sprayed until all the fruit is harvested.

General care   Tie in the young canes of blackberries to ensure that they are not broken.

Prune loganberries by cutting out at ground level the canes which have just borne fruit, and train in the new young canes produced this year in their place.

Prune plums if necessary, cutting out only the weak, diseased or overcrowded branches.

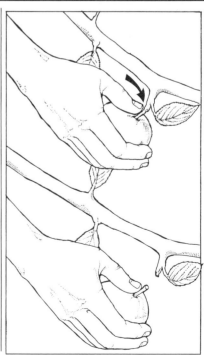

To pick apples and pears, place the thumb against the stalk and pull gently.

September

Plants of the Month

This is the month when the garden should be full of mellow colours—the yellows and bronzes of the changing leaves and flowers such as rudbeckia and helianthus—and to contrast with these the soft pinks and blues of the erigerons, ceanothus and hibiscus continuing from August to be joined by the lovely pink sedums which can also be relied on to attract the butterflies.

SHRUBS

Caryopteris   Small shrub growing to 1 m (3 ft) or so with clusters of blue flowers. Prefers a sunny position and well drained soil and should be cut back hard in March.

Erica (Heather)   For a lime-free sandy peat and open position there are a number of ericas which will be in flower this month. The varieties of *Erica cinerea* bell heather, provide some of the brightest colour, these include C. D. Eason, red-pink, Purple Beauty, White Dale and Foxhollow Mahogany, and some have the added interest of golden or reddish foliage.

Also flowering now are varieties of *E. vagans* the Cornish heath, Mrs D. F. Maxwell has deep rose flowers, St Keverne, salmon pink. Clip all these heathers over in March or April.

Fuchsia   Some varieties of fuchsia are easily grown outdoors in a sunny or partially shady position and most soils. The growth may be cut back to ground level in the winter but it shoots up again in spring to form a bush between 60 cm and 1 m (2 and 3 ft) high.

Tamarix (Tamarisk)   This deciduous shrub carries its plumy sprays of reddish or pink flowers from July to September depending on variety and thrives in well drained soils and a sunny position. It grows especially well in coastal districts. *Tamarix gallica* and *T. anglica* are the latest flowering kinds. No pruning necessary but they can be cut back hard in March or April to improve the flower quality. Cut back previous year's growth to within a few inches of the main stems.

FLOWERING PLANTS

Anemone   The perennial Japanese anemone carries its white to deep pink flowers this month and grows up to 1·25 m (4 ft) high in most soils and a sunny or shady position. It does not like to be disturbed after planting but can be increased by division in spring when necessary. September

Charm, pink and Louise Uhink, white are especially good.

Dahlia   With flowers in all colours except blue and many sizes, this must be considered one of the most useful of garden plants. There are so many varieties ranging in height from 30 cm to 2 m (1 to 6 ft) that making a choice is difficult. Dahlias need a rich well cultivated soil and sunny position. The roots must be lifted and stored dry through the winter.

Geum   Easily grown with a long flowering season from June to September, geums thrive in a well drained soil and warm sunny place. The flowers in yellow, orange or red are carried on 30- to 60- cm (1- to 2- ft) stems according to variety. Look for Mrs Bradshaw, scarlet, Lady Strathedon, yellow and *G. borisii* with orange-red flowers. All are perennials.

Helianthus (Sunflower)   It is the perennial kinds which flower at this time of the year and all will grow in a reasonably well-drained soil and open position. Heights vary from 1.25 to 2 m (4 to 7 ft) according to variety and flowers are in shades of yellow. Loddon Gold with double flowers is especially recommended.

1 Japanese anemones, *Anemone japonica*
2 Dahlia variety Goody Goody
3 *Rudbeckia* Marmalade
4 Stonecrop, *Sedum telephium*, a variety with deep pink flowers
5 Spitfire, a variety of crocosmia. These are sometimes called montbretia

Rudbeckia (Coneflower) Sun lovers which will grow in most soils, the perennial varieties have daisy-type flowers in yellow or orange often with a raised central cone which may differ in colour. Heights vary from about 30 cm to 2 m (1 to 6 ft).

Sedum (Stonecrop) Good border and rock garden plants which grow up to about 60 cm (2 ft) tall depending on variety. Best in well drained soil in an open position. *Sedum spectabile* and Autumn Joy are especially fine kinds, both with pink flowers. Others have white, yellow or reddish coloured flowers.

Solidago (Golden Rod) Easily grown in most soils and a fairly open position, the perennial golden rod has sprays of small yellow flowers in late summer and early autumn. Varieties vary in height from 30 cm to 2 m (1 to 6 ft).

BULBS

Crocosmia This enjoys sun, warmth and a well drained soil and produces its yellow, orange or coppery-red flowers in 60-cm to 1 m (2 to 3 ft) spikes in August and September. The corms can either be lifted after flowering and stored dry throughout the winter or left in the ground and given some protection.

Cyclamen Two species flowering in summer and autumn are *Cyclamen europaeum* with crimson flowers and *C. neapolitanum* with pink or white flowers. Each grows about 15 cm (6 in) high and prefers a peaty soil in partial shade.

Leucojum The autumn snowflake, *Leucojum autumnale*, has small pinkish-white flowers on 15-cm (6-in) stems. Bulbs can be planted to 10 cm (4 in) deep in July in very well drained soil and a sunny sheltered position.

FRUIT IN THE GARDEN

Broad beans, French beans, runner beans, beetroot, broccoli, cabbage, carrots, cauliflower, celery, ridge cucumbers, leaf beet, leeks, lettuce, marrows, parsnips, peas, potatoes, radish, spinach, sweet corn, tomatoes, turnips.

VEGETABLES IN THE GARDEN

Apples, blackberries, cherries, late blackcurrants, pears, plums, raspberries.

INSIDE

Achimenes Small plants with trumpet-shaped flowers in white, pink, red or purple which occur from June to September depending on when the small tubers are started into growth between January and May. No special treatment required.

VEGETABLES IN THE GREENHOUSE

Cucumbers, tomatoes

September

Inside

From now on we must expect frost, and this means that before the end of the month, all the frost-tender plants which have been out in the garden will have to be rehoused.

If the greenhouse was shaded during the summer with permanent shading painted on to the glass, what remains should now be washed off.

Sowing   Continue to sow annuals for spring flowering in the greenhouse. Prick out those which have germinated into 3-in pots and keep them as near to the glass as possible. They need cool, light conditions to grow well, and it may be best to put them in the garden frame for a few weeks.

Cuttings   This is a good time to take cuttings of fuchsias and geranium, in fact, I much prefer to see the majority of the geranium cuttings taken and put in before the middle of the month.

The regal pelargonium cuttings taken in August should be potted on into $3\frac{1}{2}$-in pots and the geranium cuttings rooted out of doors should be lifted and potted up. All these should be thoroughly watered after potting, and from then on watered with the utmost care. I prefer to leave them until the compost in the pots is really dry before watering again.

All the half-ripe cuttings taken earlier in the year should now be potted into $3\frac{1}{2}$-in pots. When well established in these they can be plunged in the garden for planting next year.

Begonias and gloxinias
When the tuberous begonias and gloxinias have finished flowering, they should be placed under the greenhouse staging with the pots laid on their sides to allow the plants to dry off.

Carnations   Bring in any plants which have been standing in the garden frame.

Chrysanthemums   The late-flowering chrysanthemums growing in pots outside should be fed twice a week with liquid fertiliser. They will need to be well tied to canes to give support to the shoots which might be broken off by strong winds.

Spray them at intervals with a combined insecticide and fungicide to keep them free from insect pests and mildew. Spraying does not generally seem to be effective against earwigs, and to prevent damage from these it is advisable to dust the young shoots with an insecticidal powder. Earwigs affecting plants at this time of year can cause many disfigured and distorted blooms.

At the very end of the month it is time to think about taking the plants inside. It is always risky to leave them outside in October because of the danger of frosts.

Cyclamen   If these have been kept in the garden frame, they must be moved into the greenhouse before the end of the month. When the weather is mild at night I like to take off the frame lights because I find the plants enjoy the dew on the leaves. Put aside some of the best plants and allow these to flower to provide autumn colour in the greenhouse, but continue to pull off the flower buds from the remainder.

Primulas   Feed regularly with liquid fertiliser until the flower buds have formed.

General care   Clear away the tomatoes and cucumbers as early in the month as possible to make space for the many plants which have to come inside. I like to wash the glass and the framework inside before putting any more plants in position.

Bulbs in pots and bowls
Early September is the time to think about potting up those bulbs you wish to grow for Christmas and later winter flowering. The prepared hyacinths are put in at the beginning of the month, and the daffodils and other narcissi, crocuses, chionodoxas, scillas and other early bulbs towards the end of the month.

After potting, keep the containers in a cool dark place for eight weeks or so to encourage the formation of the roots. When shoots are seen the containers can be brought out into the light, but they must be kept cool until the flower buds are well formed. Failure to do this may result in no flowers developing.

HOUSE PLANTS

Lift and rehouse all those plants which have been standing in the garden. If any have been plunged in soil, I think it is advisable to knock them from their pots and check for the presence of earthworms or other pests. If in doubt, repot in fresh compost.

Check for pests and spray with an insecticide before bringing them back into the house.

Potting up bulbs

For display indoors it is usual to pot the bulbs in ornamental bowls without drainage holes, and since ordinary potting compost becomes sour in undrained containers, it is advisable to use a proprietary bulb fibre. The fibre must first be thoroughly moistened as it is difficult to get it wet after potting is completed. Squeeze out any surplus moisture and put a layer into the bottom of the bowl, adjusting the quantity so that the tips of the bulbs are just above the level of the rim of the bowl.

Hyacinth bulbs should be placed about 2·5 cm (1 in) apart, those of narcissi can nearly touch whilst tulip bulbs need to be 2·5 to 5 cm (1 to 2 in) apart. Pack more fibre around the bulbs,

leaving the tips showing above the surface and leave enough space below the rim for watering.

Keep the bowls in a cool dark cupboard or out of doors covered with old sacks or fertiliser bags. Keep an eye on them regularly and check to see if any water is required.

When the shoots are about an inch high the bowls can be brought into a cool light place to make further growth. Do not bring them into a warm room until the flower buds can be seen.

Special pots can be obtained for potting crocuses and these make an especially attractive display. The corms are positioned, one by each hole, as the pots are filled and as a finishing touch more corms are planted to fill the top opening. It is especially

important to keep crocuses very cool when growth begins as in higher temperatures they make a lot of foliage at the expense of flowers.

To get a greater concentration of colour, daffodils can be planted in two layers in large pots or tubs (bottom right). The pots should have drainage holes and an ordinary potting compost can be used. Place some crocks in the bottom, then a layer of compost and the first row of bulbs. Cover the bulbs with compost so that the tips are just showing and position the second row so that the bulbs are between the tips of the first row. Add more compost to bring the level to just below the rim of the pot and firm.

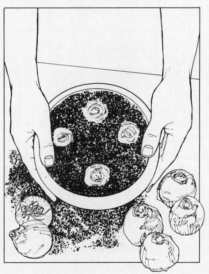

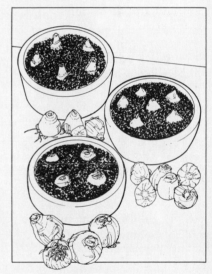

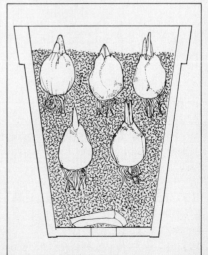

93

CHECK LIST
Plant trees and shrubs
Make hardwood cuttings
Make rock gardens
Plant spring-flowering
    plants
Plant bulbs
Divide hardy border plants
Lift dahlias and chrysanthemums
Plant cabbage
Store fruit

October

'In October
dung your field
And your land
its wealth shall yield'

Although this is one of the most important months of the year for planting trees and shrubs, there is not the urgency about garden tasks that exists in spring and early summer—principally because things are not growing as rapidly as they do at that time of the year.

The division and replanting of the hardy border plants can be done now, but if there are a lot of autumn-flowering plants around, such as the Michaelmas daisies, it is better left to the late winter. I prefer to do it then anyway.

A word about buying plants, this is usually done in one of two ways: by mail order from a reputable nursery firm, or from a retail outlet such as a garden centre or store. Trees and shrubs may be offered for sale as container-grown specimens, in which case they can be bought and planted at any time of the year, or as bare-rooted or balled specimens which are available only at the orthodox planting season from October to March.

Bare-rooted trees and shrubs must be planted as soon after arrival as possible and the roots should be soaked in a bucket of water if they are at all dry. Trees and shrubs that have been balled, and this may well be the case with conifers and evergreens, can be left for a little longer if necessary. After positioning the plant in the hole, the sacking covering the rootball may be left in place to retain as much soil as possible around the roots. The hardy border plants and rock plants are always available as pot-grown specimens and these, too, can be planted throughout the year although it is always wise to avoid very dry spells. When choosing plants for the garden, it is important to take into account the type of soil you have. Some, such as azaleas and rhododendrons require an acid soil, whilst others such as the pinks and clematis are better on an alkaline one.

October

Outside

TREES AND SHRUBS
This is a good month to plant conifers and other evergreens and all deciduous plants.

Now is the time when it is possible to take hardwood cuttings of all shrubs including roses, and conifers.

Choose a firm young shoot and remove any soft wood from the tip. Trim the end and remove any lower leaves. When completed, the cutting should be about 23 cm (9 in) long. Dip the ends in hormone rooting powder and line out the cuttings in a shallow trench with some sand in the bottom. Firm carefully into position. Leave undisturbed for a year before planting out.

FLOWERS
Planting   The main job this month is to put in all the spring-flowering plants. Make the soil firm by treading before planting, and sprinkle bonemeal over the surface at the rate of a handful to the square yard.

I like to plant both polyanthus and wallflowers with tulips inbetween, using the early single varieties between the polyanthus and the taller Darwins among the wallflowers.

Other plants to go in now include forget-me-nots, again mixed with tulips, cheiranthus (the Siberian wallflower—if cut back after flowering, this will flower again later in the summer), *Bellis perennis* in its various forms, winter-flowering pansies, Sweet Williams, Canterbury bells and foxgloves. I allow the foxgloves to seed themselves between shrubs and other plants. At this time of the year I lift some of the self-sown seedlings and plant them where I want them.

When planting bellis—the double daisy—it is advisable to keep them away from the grass edges because they will produce seeds, causing masses of daisy seedlings to grow in the lawn.

Tubs and containers   These can also be planted now and I suggest that the compost— John Innes potting compost No. 3—be renewed every three years. For a colourful and long-lasting effect I suggest planting a mixture of polyanthus, wallflowers, daffodil Golden Harvest, early double-flowering tulips, and a few large-flowered crocus.

Bulb planting   Complete the bulb planting now with such things as *Iris reticulata*, chionodoxa, snowdrops, *Fritillaria meleagris*, miniature daffodils and narcissi— including *cyclamineus*, W.P. Milner, *bulbocodium*, February Gold and *triandrus albus*— and crocus varieties such as *tomasinianus*, Whitewell Purple, Snow Bunting, Golden Golden, E.P. Bowles and Cream Beauty.

This is the best time to do any naturalising of bulbs, see p. 89.

Dividing plants   I prefer to lift my hardy border plants in March or early April, but there are those who like to get the job done at this time of year. Generally speaking most of these plants are all the better for being divided every three years.

Lifting these plants provides an opportunity to enrich the soil which will have become

Now is a good time to make hardwood cuttings of shrubs, trees, roses, gooseberries and currants. The leaves should be left on evergreen kinds.

Root clumps of hardy border plants can be prised apart.

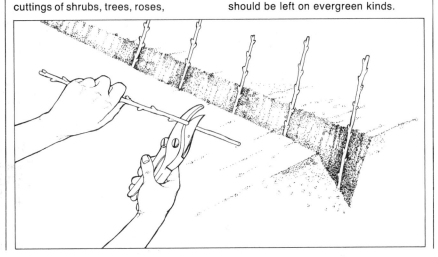

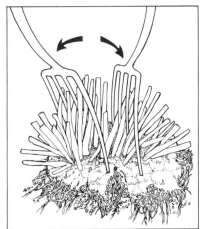

impoverished. Manure, garden compost or peat can be mixed in as the soil is turned over. Bonemeal, sprinkled over the surface at the rate of a handful to the square metre (yard), will mix into the soil as the holes are made for replanting the divided plants.

It is essential to ensure that the soil is pressed firmly around the roots of the divisions. At the same time, any hardy border plants raised from seed can be put in.

Now is also the time to continue tidying the border, cutting back plants and removing old stems and leaves.
Dahlias Cut down the top of each plant to within 15 to 23 cm (6 to 9 in) of the soil and label the stump. The roots are then lifted carefully and placed under the greenhouse staging or in a shed. Store them stem downwards so that any moisture in the hollow stems will drain away. If the stems are not dried in this way, a mould is likely to form which will cause roots and buds to rot.
Chrysanthemums The roots of the outdoor flowering chrysanthemums wanted for producing cuttings early next year must also be lifted. After cutting off the tops, these can be lifted and placed into boxes and covered with old compost or peat and sand. Keep in a cool place until February, when they can be taken into the greenhouse.
The rock garden This is a good month in which to renovate an existing garden, or establish a new one. It does not have to be elaborate: six or eight carefully selected stones placed in position can offer scope for growing a range of the more choice small plants. Choose an open sunny position as all these plants like free drainage. Fill the pockets (the flat planting ledges between the

Making a rock garden

Choose a sunny position away from overhanging trees and make sure that the drainage is good.

The kind of rocks used should fit in naturally with the surroundings if possible—those with well marked strata are best as these will help to make the rock garden look natural.

Each piece of rock should be firmly embedded in soil and positioned so that the natural lines or strata run in the same direction.

When building the rock garden on a flat area, some larger stones will be required to make the levels and create a series of ledges. The soil must be packed around the rocks so that these are completely stable.

rocks) with a mixture of three parts garden soil, one part peat, one part sand and a little bonemeal.

Protect any very choice plants with a pane of glass supported on wires.

THE LAWN
Raking the lawn is a job I like to get done at this time of year.

It gives the grass a good combing, pulls out dead grasses and rubbish and moss too. After raking, topdress with a mixture of peat and sand.

This month often sees the last cut of the year, although this will depend on the weather.

This is a good time to make lawns from turf. See page 29 for instructions.

October

Plants of the Month

This can be one of the most colourful months of the year in the garden, with rich autumn tints developing on many trees and shrubs. Among the best for this are *Rhus typhina*, cotinus, the Japanese maples, deciduous azaleas, some of the cherries and liquidambar.

TREES

Liquidambar   Although it may be erratic in colouring, when it does turn the leaves shade to red and purple and are very striking. It requires a deep, fairly moist soil and sunny position and is not good on chalk.

Metasequoia (Dawn Redwood)   One of the deciduous conifers, metasequoia has a graceful habit and feathery foliage which turns pinkish-brown in the autumn. It needs an open sunny position and good, moist soil, and may grow to 21 m (70 ft).

Prunus (Cherry)   Two cherries in particular are noted for their autumn foliage colour: Sargent's cherry, *Prunus sargentii*, 5·5 m (18 ft), and *P. hillieri* Spire, 6 m (21 ft), which has an upright growing habit. Cherries grow on most soils and in an open sunny position.

Rhus typhina (Stag's Horn Sumach)   Small tree or large shrub which will grow to 3·5 m (12 ft) in an ordinary soil and sunny position. The fern-like leaves turn scarlet and yellow in autumn. Side shoots may be cut back in late winter.

SHRUBS and CLIMBERS

Acer (Japanese maples)   There are many good varieties of *Acer palmatum* which grow slowly to between 1 and 3·5 m (3 to 12 ft), and prefer a well drained soil and sheltered position. They all have decorative foliage which in many is especially effective in autumn. No pruning required.

Cotinus coggygria (Smoke Tree)   Closely related to *Rhus typhina*, but with round leaves which colour well in the autumn. There is also a most effective purple-leaved form. Best for a sunny position and well drained soil where it will grow to about 2·5 m (8 ft). Regular pruning unnecessary, but it can be cut back in spring if space is limited.

Parthenocissus (Virginia Creeper)   The most magnificent of all climbers as it colours to a spectacular scarlet and orange in autumn. It needs ample space and will grow in partial shade or full sun. Prune as necessary to reduce size in autumn.

FLOWERING PLANTS

Aster (Michaelmas daisies)   Very useful plants with many varieties, ranging in height from 15 cm to 1·5 m (6 in to 5 ft), and in flower colour from blue through purple, pink and crimson to white. The main flowering season is September/October, and they are not fussy about soil or position which can be sunny or lightly shaded.

Cortaderia (Pampas Grass)   Vigorous, decorative grass growing in clumps which produce elegant flower plumes in autumn that may be anything up to 2 m (7 ft) tall. It grows best in a warm sunny place and well drained soil and dislikes disturbance.

Schizostylis (Kaffir Lily)   Spikes of red or pink flowers up to 75 cm (2½ ft) tall are produced from September to November and provide valuable autumn colour. Best in milder areas and needing well drained soil and a warm sunny position. It may need winter protection.

1 Japanese maples, *Acer palmatum*
2 Michaelmas daisies, *Aster* Picture
3 Pampas Grass, cortaderia
4 The meadow saffron, *Colchicum autumnale*
5 Saintpaulia, African violet

BULBS

Amaryllis (Belladonna Lily, Jersey Lily)   Not a true lily, but the pink or white flowers are trumpet shaped. Amaryllis is not completely hardy and must have a warm sunny position near the base of a wall. In cold areas a covering of peat or sand is necessary to protect the bulbs in winter. When planting the bulbs, make sure that they are only just covered with soil—deep planting can prevent flowering.

Colchicum (Meadow Saffron, Autumn Crocus) Flowering in September and October and not related to the crocus, the colchicums do best in rock gardens or at the front of borders in a good soil and fairly sunny position. They can also be naturalised in grass. The large pink, mauve or white flowers are produced before the leaves. Height 15 cm (6 in) or so. Plant in July or August and cover the bulbs with 5 cm (2 in) of soil.

Nerine (Guernsey Lily)   The flower cluster is produced in September and October before the leaves, and the colour range is mainly from pink to scarlet. Only suitable for growing outdoors in the mildest areas, where they must have a position near the foot of a south-facing wall. Plant the bulbs in July only just covering them with soil and provide winter protection.

VEGETABLES IN THE GARDEN

Jerusalem artichokes, broad beans, French beans, runner beans, beetroot, broccoli, Brussels sprouts, cabbage, carrots, cauliflower, celery, leeks, lettuce parsnips, peas, spinach, swede, sweetcorn, tomatoes, turnips.

FRUIT IN THE GARDEN

Apples, pears, plums, quince, raspberries.

INSIDE

Exacum   Excellent pot plant with fragrant lilac flowers, each with a yellow centre. Sow seed in a temperature of 15°C (59°F) in March, prick out and pot on as necessary until plants are in 4- or 5-in pots. Water moderately throughout.

Saintpaulia (African Violets)   These lovely little plants have hairy leaves and flower clusters in all shades of pink, blue, purple, cerise as well as white. They are ideal for growing as house or conservatory plants as, under good conditions, they will flower for much of the year. They need a humid atmosphere and careful watering.

VEGETABLES

In the vegetable garden, it is time for the final harvesting of carrots, beetroot, swedes, and turnips.

Give celery a final earthing up, and draw up a little soil along each side of the leeks.

Clear away the remains of the runner beans and put them on the compost heap, then brush the soil from the bottom of the supporting canes before putting these away. If canes are stored in the dry they will last much longer.

Winter lettuce can now be planted 15 cm (6 in) apart in a shallow drill. It is advisable to put down some slug bait, but make sure this is protected by a tile so that birds and pets cannot get at it. Cloches can be put over these lettuce later in the year.

Spring cabbage should also be planted now. Set these 23 cm (9 in) apart and plant them very firmly. In the spring, every other one will be taken out for eating when they have formed a reasonable amount of leaf. Those that remain will then be 45 cm (18 in) apart.

Feed Brussels sprouts and winter cabbage with general fertiliser. Remove any yellowing leaves from the sprouts.

Lift the remainder of the maincrop potatoes. Allow them to dry off and store in paper or hessian sacks.

FRUIT

Clean up and hoe between all the fruit and plant new bushes and trees.

Take hardwood cuttings of gooseberries as described earlier for shrubs, but remove all the buds except the top three or four, to ensure that bushes are

Store only sound, unmarked apples, wrapping them individually and placing them in boxes.

grown on a short stem or 'leg'.

Storing October sees the completion of all the apple and pear picking. Any apples which have been marked or damaged should be put aside for immediate use as they will not store. The sound fruits can be placed in single layers in trays; I like to use tomato trays for this because the raised corners allow for free circulation of air between stacked boxes. Whilst it is still possible to get the waxed paper squares for wrapping apples, they are not readily available, and I find

a good white tissue paper does the job almost as well. Stack the trays in the coolest place you have.

Pears can be stored in a similar way to apples, but they must be kept where they can be inspected at regular intervals. Pears must be used as soon as they ripen—in a matter of a day they will go sleepy (brown and mushy) and are spoiled.

When setting out young cabbage plants, firm them in so well that they cannot be pulled out again, and water after planting.

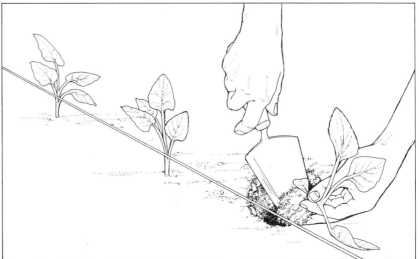

Inside

Ventilate the greenhouse well now to keep the air moving and prevent too stagnant an atmosphere occurring, which might encourage diseases. Some heat may be required if the weather is very frosty.

Potting There is plenty to be done in the greenhouse with fuchsia and geranium cuttings to be potted, also calceolarias and *Primula malacoides*.

The schizanthus and other spring-flowering annuals should be ready now for stopping. Take out the young tips to encourage the formation of sturdy, bushy plants. These will soon need potting on into 5-in pots.

Both Beauty of Nice and East Lothian stocks are ready for potting on too. These, like the schizanthus, must be kept growing slowly in cool airy conditions, and need even more care in watering as the days get shorter, and the outside temperatures become lower.

Begonias and gloxinias Once the foliage has withered on the tuberous begonias and gloxinias, the tubers can be knocked from their pots, shaken free of compost, dusted with flowers of sulphur and stored in a cool, dust-free atmosphere.

Calceolarias Pot on into 6-in pots.

Chrysanthemums These are likely to be growing fast and must be kept as cool as possible. Nip off any side buds that are produced and reduce the number of shoots to 10 to 12 on a plant. Spray again with a combined insecticide and fungicide, water regularly and feed twice a week until the colour of the petals shows.

Cinerarias These need careful watering; they must be neither too dry nor too wet. Watch out for the silvery trails on the leaves which indicate the presence of the grubs of the leaf miner. By turning the leaf over it is possible to see where the grub is, and this can be pinched between thumb and finger to prevent it doing further damage.

Cyclamen Continue to pull off the cyclamen flower buds until the end of October, and do the same on *Primula obconica*.

Fuchsia The large fuchsia plants which provided flowers during the summer need to be given less water from now on, thus forcing the plants to rest until pruning and potting early next year.

Bulbs in bowls and pots The hyacinths specially prepared for Christmas were planted last month. Early this month is the time to plant early double and early single-flowering tulips in pots and bowls and more daffodils and narcissi and hyacinths to provide a continuity of early indoor flowers.

Check to see if bulbs planted earlier need any water—they should not be allowed to dry out.

HOUSE PLANTS

Cut back on watering and stop feeding. Because of the dry atmospheric conditions which exist in most homes it is advisable to increase humidity around plants by either plunging them in damp peat, standing them on moist gravel, or spraying them over with water.

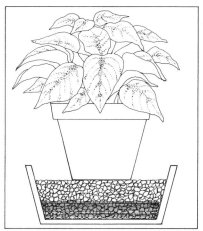

To keep house plants growing well in a heated room, improve the humidity by using one of the methods shown above.

November

'If there's ice in November
that will bear a duck
There'll be nothing after,
but sludge and muck'

November brings to mind fallen leaves and bonfires, although it is
probably more useful as far as the garden is concerned
to make the leaves into compost. It also sees the beginning of
the winter digging, and I well remember working in a
large walled kitchen garden and having to double dig or
trench for various crops—that really was a back-breaking
task. There is very little of this done these days, and I
am of the opinion that it is sufficient if the soil is well
turned over to the depth of the spade. But unless one is
accustomed to digging, it can be hard work and should be done
a little at a time. If the garden soil is inclined to be of a
heavy nature then it is essential for it to be dug over and
left in large lumps to expose as much of it as possible to the
beneficial effects of the weather. As you dig, remove the
roots of any perennial weeds. Before doing any digging
it is advisable to have a plan in mind or on paper, of where
you intend to sow or plant the various crops next spring.
If this is not done you may well be digging in manure
or garden compost in those areas where parsnips,
carrots and other root crops are to be grown.

With our minds turning unavoidably to winter and the cold
weather it is advisable to think about putting some form of
protection around any newly planted conifers, otherwise the tips of
the branches may turn brown. A screen made of old sacks firmly
secured to stakes on the windward side of the plant will give
protection from strong winds. Sharp frosts may also be a
problem, and to give protection from these polythene sheeting can
be wrapped around the plant or a large polythene bag can be put
right over the plant and secured around the stem. This may be left
in place for most of the winter without the plant inside coming to
any harm.

During the first winter, strong winds and frosts may loosen any
newly planted shrubs as these will not have rooted into the soil.
I make a point of going round the garden at regular intervals to
check and refirm them if necessary.

CHECK LIST

Plant trees and shrubs
Plant hedges
Plant lilies
Gather leaves onto compost
heap
Fork lawn
Dig vegetable garden
Prune fruit trees and bushes

Outside

TREES AND SHRUBS

Planting When I started gardening, now more years ago than I wish to remember, I was taught that the orthodox planting season was from November to March, as this was when most trees, shrubs and roses, as well as other plants, were more or less dormant. And if planting was done in November there was a much better chance of success: the soil was still reasonably warm and the plants had a chance to make some new roots before really bad weather set in.

These days many shrubs, roses and trees are grown in containers and can be planted at almost any time of the year. This has changed the fashions and methods of gardening considerably. I must say that there is a greater chance of success when trees and shrubs are planted from containers because there is little or no disturbance to the roots. However, these need to be planted with the same care as those with bare roots. It is essential that the roots are not allowed to become dry. If they seem dry, place them in water for several hours so they are well soaked before planting.

When planting conifers and other evergreens it is as well to remember that the roots should not be placed too deeply in the soil. The top 20 to 25 cm (8 to 10 in) is the fertile soil and the roots should not be deeper than this.

To assist good root formation, they need a good rooting medium with some peat or composted bark mixed in. They must be planted firmly, and if they are more than 45 to 60 cm (18 to 24 in) in height, a cane or a stake support is necessary to prevent them from being blown backwards and forwards, which can result in irreparable damage to the roots.

Roses Rose bushes planted in November are usually better than those which are put in after Christmas, and give a better display the following summer. Make the hole large enough for the roots to be spread out, and deep enough so that when planting is finished, the point at which the rose has been budded onto the rootstock is at, or just below, the surface of the soil. Make the soil really firm by treading so that the whole root system is in direct contact with the soil.

Although bushes are not pruned hard back when planting is done, the tops should be shortened to prevent them from being blown backwards and forwards by the wind.

Making compost There will be plenty of leaves to collect during the next few weeks, especially where they are lying thickly on grassed areas or covering any smaller plants on the rock garden. If you have a pool, pull out as many as possible with a wire rake because too many leaves decaying in the water tend to make the pool stagnant, and this is not good for the fish.

There are those who say that certain kinds of leaves should not be put onto the compost heap. I never keep any back, the only difference is that some kinds of leaves take longer to break down than others.

FLOWERS

There is still time to plant tulips, lily of the valley and all the spring-flowering plants.

Planting lilies November is also the time for planting most of the hardy lilies. These like a well-worked soil with good drainage, and I like to set each bulb on a little sand in the bottom of each planting hole. Plant the bulbs in groups of three or four, spacing them a few inches apart within each group.

Planting non-stem-rooting lilies on a layer of sand.

Some lilies form roots on the lower part of the stems and these must be planted more deeply—20 to 23 cm (8 to 9 in) —than the non-stem-rooting kinds at 13 to 15 cm (5 to 6 in).

Hardy border plants A few of the border plants, such as the red hot pokers and gunnera, are slightly tender and may not survive hard frosts. These should be protected now by tying any remaining leaves over the centre of the plants and covering them with bracken or straw.

Planting

Now we are well into the planting season and many shrubs, conifers and roses will be available growing in containers. When planting these, first remove the container carefully. Then, without disturbing the ball of roots, place it in a hole, return the soil and firm.

Planting hedges The method is much the same as for planting individual shrubs but the position of the hedge may be marked out with canes or a line first.

If the plants are to be placed 60 cm (2 ft) or more apart, they are put in individual holes, but if the recommended planting distance is less than this then it is easier to take out a trench 38 to 45 cm (15 to 18 in) wide to run the length of the intended hedge. Whichever the method used, the planting must be firm and each shrub must be staked or tied onto a training wire to prevent windrock while the roots are establishing themselves.

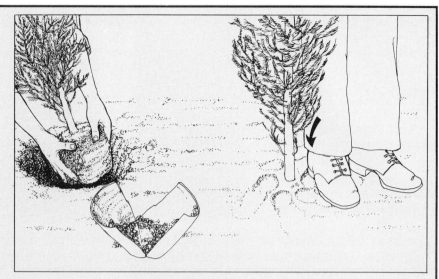

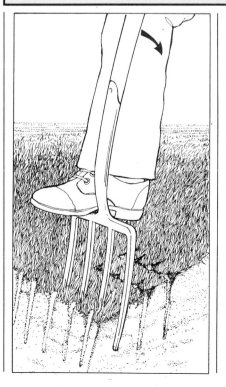

Forking the lawn helps to aerate the soil and improves the growth of grass roots.

At this time of year I usually put cloches over the Christmas roses not so much to protect them from frost and cold, but to bring the flowers along earlier and to prevent the petals being splashed.

THE LAWN

The lawn is now ready for forking or spiking. I have a spiked roller which helps on a large area of lawn, but I am never satisfied that spiking is as good as forking with a garden fork. This is pushed in at intervals of 8 to 10 cm (3 to 4 in) and to the same depth, and the handle is pulled slightly backwards, cracking the surface and helping to loosen the compacted soil.

Forking should be followed by topdressing with a mixture of soil, peat and sand in equal parts. I allow a large shovelful for each square metre (yard). Apply the topdressing when the grass is dry so that it can be pushed about with the back of the rake to find its way down into the grass; at no time must it be left lying thickly on top, otherwise the grass will turn yellow and die.

This is still a good time to lay turf.

Clean and grease the mower and store it away in a dry place. Now is the best time to get it overhauled and have the blades sharpened.

November

Plants of the Month

With the leaves falling from the trees and taking with them the last of the autumn colours, the garden would now be looking very naked if it were not for the evergreen trees and shrubs. A few conifers and other evergreens situated at focal points in the garden can do much to provide a basic foundation for the other more seasonal plants. Also coming into their own in the last part of the year will be the various berry-producing plants.

CONIFERS

Juniper   The Irish Juniper, *J. communis* Hibernica, has glaucous foliage and a columnar habit and grows slowly to about 3·5 m (12 ft). It likes an open sunny position and does well on a soil containing lime or chalk. By contrast, *J. squamata* Blue Carpet is a prostrate variety which forms an intense silver-blue carpet.
Picea (Spruce)   This is the genus which gives us the Christmas tree, but a more attractive garden plant is the slow-growing *Picea pungens* Kosteri, the blue spruce, which makes a most handsome small tree with rich blue-grey foliage. Give it good deep soil and an open sunny position.
Thuja (Arbor-vitae)   The slow-growing *Thuja occidentalis* Rheingold makes a compact pyramid with golden summer foliage which changes to bronze in winter. Another good thuja is *T. plicata* Zebrina which grows to about 9 m (30 ft) and has foliage banded in green and yellow. All thujas will grow in ordinary well drained soil and a position in sun or shade.

TREES AND SHRUBS

Berberis (Barberry)   It is the deciduous kinds which produce good crops of scarlet or coral berries in the autumn, and many have lovely autumn colour to recommend them further. All thrive on dry sandy or chalky soils and grow anywhere except in heavy shade.
Pernettya   Small evergreen shrub growing to around 1 m (3 ft) with white flowers in early summer, but most notable for the large berries, that are pink, purple, white, black or crimson according to species, which are produced from now on. To get the berries both male and female forms must be grown. Best in lime-free peaty soils and sun or light shade. Prune in spring if necessary to restrict growth.

1 *Picea pungens* Kosteri
2 *Thuja occidentalis* Rheingold
3 *Pyracantha rogersiana* Flava
4 Cyclamen
5 *Primula obconica*

and white flowers appearing from March to April which are followed by red berries. It grows to an average of 1 to 1·25 m (3 to 4 ft) in sun or shade and almost any soil. There are both male and female forms and although normally both must be grown if you want the berries, it is now possible to buy forms which have the male and female flowers on the same bush.

Sorbus (Mountain Ash)   These trees flower in May and June and then in the autumn produce brightly coloured berries and richly tinted foliage. They grow best on a light, well drained soil and open sunny position.

BORDER PLANTS

Physalis (Chinese Lantern)   A perennial plant for a well drained soil and a sunny position that will die if it is at all waterlogged in winter. The white flowers occur in summer, but it is the inflated orange lanterns containing the cherry-like fruits which are so effective.

VEGETABLES IN THE GARDEN

Jerusalem artichoke, broccoli, Brussels sprouts, cabbage, cauliflower, celery, kale, leaf beet, leeks, lettuce, parsnips, Savoy cabbage, spinach, swede.

INSIDE

Chrysanthemums   The greenhouse chrysanthemums should now be providing flowers for cutting. A good range of varieties to grow are the Loveliness kinds, these come in a variety of colours and are the easiest to manage.

Cyclamen   The first of the greenhouse cyclamen should also be coming into flower. These lovely plants have distinctive flowers with reflexed petals in a wide range of shades from pure white to crimson or magenta. Many also have their leaves attractively marked in silver. Water carefully and keep fairly cool.

Primula obconica   This is the first of the greenhouse primulas to flower, and the colour range includes the pinks, reds, mauves and blues. Give plants light and keep fairly cool. Water moderately, taking care not to splash the leaves.

Tradescantia   There are various kinds of this useful trailing plant which can be relied upon to give foliage interest throughout the year. It is easily propagated from cuttings which will root readily. The variegated kinds must be kept in good light.

Prunus (Cherry)   The cherries are mostly thought of as spring-flowering trees but there is an autumn and winter-flowering form—*P. subhirtella autumnalis*, the rosebud cherry—which produces its white or pale pink flowers from now on. It grows to around 6 m (20 ft) high and has a very beautiful weeping form which flowers in March and April.

Pyracantha (Firethorn)   These are showy evergreen shrubs with white flowers in May and June, followed by masses of red and yellow berries in autumn and winter. They grow easily in any soil, in shade or sun and can also be trained against walls. Most grow to about 2·5 m (8 ft) high. *P. coccinea* Lalandei with brilliant orange-scarlet berries; *P. rogersiana* Flava with yellow berries and Orange Glow with bright orange berries are all to be recommended.

Skimmia   An evergreen with shiny green leaves

VEGETABLES

Digging Unless one is accustomed to digging, it can be hard work and should be done a little at a time. If the garden soil is inclined to be of a heavy nature, then it is essential for it to be dug over and left in large lumps to expose as much of it as possible to the effects of the weather.

Before doing any digging it is advisable to have a plan in mind, or drawn on paper, of where you intend to sow and plant the various crops next spring. If this is not done you may well be digging in manure or garden compost in areas where parsnips, carrots and other root crops will be grown.

Sowing In mild districts it is possible now to make sowings of the broad bean variety Aquadulce, and also of a hardy pea such as Pilot.

Early rhubarb To be able to enjoy those delicate pink sticks of rhubarb early in the year, lift two of the strongest roots now (those which have not been forced before), and leave them on the surface exposed to the weather for a few weeks. Then, pack them in boxes with moist soil over the roots, and keep in a dark and fairly warm place.

Root crops Look through any stored potatoes and remove any diseased specimens.

Cut down the tops of Jerusalem artichokes. If there is fear of slugs getting to the tubers, then they can be lifted and placed in a heap in a sheltered part of the garden. Lay them on newspaper, put more newspaper over them and then a good layer of sand or soil over the top.

FRUIT

Pruning Before the weather gets too cold I like to do the pruning of apples and pears where this is necessary. Cordon, espalier-trained and fan-trained trees must be pruned, but I am sure many bush and half-standard trees are spoiled by overpruning. I do the minimum amount of pruning on these, keeping the centre of the tree open, cutting out branches that cross and only shortening back some of the previous season's branches.

The cordon and other trained trees were pruned in the summer, and now the side shoots are cut back even further to two or three buds. I make a point of tying some of the young branches down to below the horizontal rather than cutting them off. This extends the fruiting area, and an amazing amount of fruit forms on these branches.

Red and white currants are also pruned now. This involves the removal of some older branches, and at the same time the main younger branches are reduced by half, and the laterals or side shoots shortened back to two or three buds.

Planting This is a good time for planting all sorts of fruit. Make sure that the soil has been well dug and some manure or garden compost worked in.

Stored fruit This should be inspected regularly and those showing signs of rot removed.

Cuttings Hardwood cuttings of black-, red and white currants can be taken now. The lower buds are removed from the red and white currants in the same way as those of gooseberry, see page 100. This will mean that the plants will develop with a short bare stem and a head of branches. In contrast, all the buds are left on hardwood cuttings of black-currants as these are grown as bushes with a number of stems coming from the roots.

Fruit pruning

This is a good time to do the main pruning of fruit trees. It is important to remember that this should never be overdone, it is always better to under- rather than overprune a bush or tree.

Once established, espalier-trained trees (below) are simply pruned by shortening all the laterals back to two or three buds from the main branches.

Shown here (below centre) is a

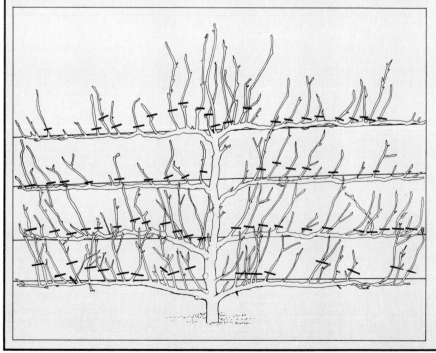

Inside

There is not much we can do in the garden after about 5 o'clock in the evening unless we have lighting in the greenhouse, something I find to be a big advantage.

It is also becoming more and more necessary to have some form of heat, and it is essential to have this thermostatically controlled to prevent wastage and thereby cut costs. Heat not only provides the temperatures the plants need, but it also keeps the air moving—so necessary at this time of year with cold damp weather outside.

For geraniums, fuchsias, regal pelargoniums and other plants which are being overwintered, a minimum temperature of 7°C (45°F) is sufficient. But at this temperature it is essential to water carefully; plants are less likely to suffer through being left dry than through being overwatered. The watering should be done early in the day if possible.

It is also important at this time of the year to look over all plants in the greenhouse and pick off any dead or yellowing leaves. If these are left they can cause the beginning of a fungal disease—botrytis—which will quickly affect the stems and cause many losses. To keep botrytis down to a minimum it is necessary to open the ventilators a little whenever the weather is reasonable.

Disbudding   Any buds which appear on the young geranium plants should be broken off; to allow these to develop retards the growth. The same applies to the young fuchsia plants.

Continue to disbud the chrysanthemums.

Feeding   The chrysanthemums will continue to need weekly feeding until the colour shows in the petals, and cyclamen will also need feeding now that they are coming into flower. I use a liquid tomato fertiliser for these because it contains extra potash, which is of more use to the plants now than nitrogen.

Cinerarias will soon be ready for a weekly feed. At this time of the year the cinerarias need very careful watering, they will flag for want of water and they will also flag if given too much. Treat them individually and water only as and when the compost feels dry.

Cuttings   Attend to any potting up of the fuchsia and pelargonium cuttings taken in September.

Bulbs in bowls   Take a look at these at weekly intervals and water if required. When they are beginning to show an inch or so of growth, they can be moved into the light. At this stage they must still be kept cool, and I like to see the flower buds above the bulbs before I move them into the warmth.

HOUSE PLANTS

Carry on with the routine care. Take measures to increase the humidity around plants (see page 101) and sponge the leaves of the large-leaved plants.

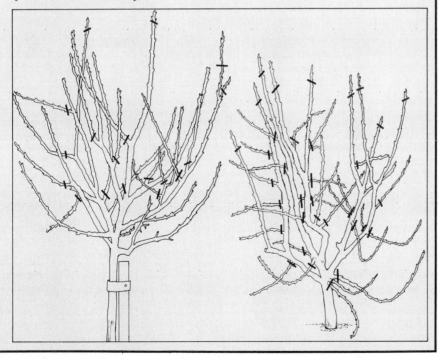

well grown bush apple tree: the main branches have been lightly cut back and the laterals or side shoots shortened to 5 to 8 cm (2 to 3 in). Continue to prune along the same lines each year and treat pears in the same way.

When pruning red and white currants (below) the leading shoots are tipped back and the laterals shortened to 2·5 cm (1 in) or so.

CHECK LIST
Tidy up tool shed
Spray fruit
Cut back chrysanthemums
Clean and store gladiolus
    corms
Lift and force mint
Bring bulbs into light
    and warmth

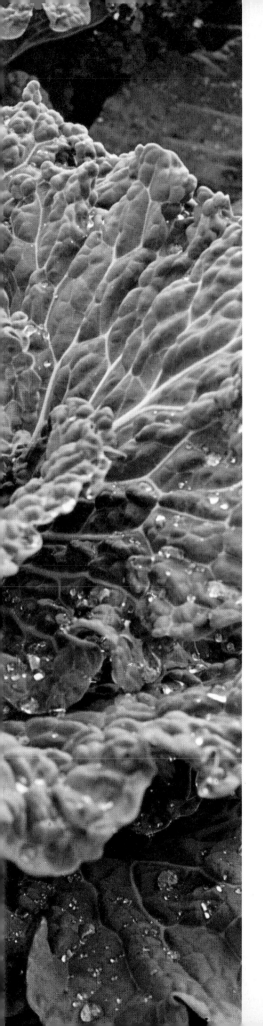

December

'Winter eateth
what summer getteth'

At this time of the year our thoughts turn to Christmas and the preparations that have to be made for the festive season. There is also Christmas shopping to be done and various gifts to be purchased. Relations and friends with a garden are, I consider, comparatively easy to please; something for the garden is always a much appreciated present. Most garden centres and shops are open every weekend and time can, I am sure, be found to browse around and choose something really suitable. So many shrubs, roses and other plants these days are sold in containers, and one of the joys of these is that they can remain for weeks before planting without coming to any harm as long as they are watered when necessary. Then there are garden tools and various pieces of garden equipment, garden books, various containers and accessories for those who are interested in flower arranging, as well as flowering plants, which in many cases are less costly and certainly last much longer than cut flowers. If there is still difficulty in making up one's mind then a gift voucher may fill the need.

To cut at least some of the costs of Christmas it is worth considering what the garden can provide in the way of decoration. From the greenhouse you may have a few last chrysanthemum blooms, possibly some cyclamen and the bulbs in bowls. From outside there should be sprays of the yellow *Jasminum nudiflorum* and perhaps one of the winter-flowering viburnums. These are better for being cut a few days before Christmas and put in water. Now is a good time to prune the holly and use the trimmings in the house. Do this carefully so that the shape of the bush is not spoiled. The delicate silvery seedpods of honesty look marvellous in a vase. Christmas roses, *Helleborus niger*, are always in demand in my house and this is why I put the cloches over them to protect them. Put the flowers in water as soon as they are cut and, if they show signs of flagging, pierce the stems in a few places with a needle. They should then perk up again and last for days.

December

Outside

With the uncertainty of the weather at this time of year it is, I consider, necessary to have a plan of the most urgent jobs to be done in the garden.

December is usually a busy month with preparations being made for Christmas, and jobs in the garden tend to be left undone. It is mostly a case of continuing with work begun last month as and when the weather allows. During spells of bad weather the tool shed can be tidied and all the tools properly cleaned and wiped over with an oily rag. Now that all tools are so expensive it is well worth taking the time to keep them in good order.

TREES AND SHRUBS

The planting of deciduous trees, shrubs and roses can continue, although not when the soil is at at all wet and sticky.

Roses Most of the late blooms will be over by now. Some people prune their hybrid tea and floribunda roses before Christmas, but I prefer only to shorten some of the taller branches to prevent the bushes from being blown backwards and forwards by the wind, which causes damage to the roots, and to leave the final pruning until March.

FLOWERS

Continue to plant the hardy lilies when weather and soil are suitable.

THE LAWN

Give the lawn a light raking or sweeping to scatter any worm casts.

VEGETABLES

If there is digging still to be done, try to do a patch each weekend—this lightens the load. In gardens of any size, say over a quarter of an acre, rotary cultivators can make this work easier. Most of these cultivate to a depth of 18 to 23 cm (7 to 9 in), and can be fitted with attachments to do other jobs such as spraying and hedge trimming.

Put cloches over the hardy winter lettuce and some of the spring cabbage to get earlier crops.

The vegetable garden will now provide cauliflowers, Brussels sprouts, parsnips, leeks and celery, with carrots, onions, beetroot and potatoes coming from storage in the garden shed.

When picking Brussels sprouts, pick from the bottom upwards, and do not remove the tops from the plants until all the sprouts have been gathered.

Fold some of the inner leaves over the cauliflower curds to protect them from the weather.

Forcing mint Lift some roots of mint, put them in a seed tray and cover them with potting compost. If kept in a cool place they will provide shoots for early picking.

FRUIT

Continue with the pruning of fruit trees.

At this time of year I make a point of looking over the apples in store every week to remove any which are showing signs of rotting or shrivelling.

Pest control Order winter wash and make a start on the spraying. This needs to be done in fairly still, dry weather, and there may not be many days to choose from. This spray will kill off moss and lichen on the trees as well as the overwintering stages of many pests, and should not be neglected.

Watch out for bird damage. A fruit cage is the ideal way of preventing this, but if the buds are sprayed with bird repellent a measure of control can be achieved. Unfortunately such repellents are washed off by rain and will have to be repeated.

Pick off and burn the enlarged buds on blackcurrants which show the presence of big bud mite.

Forcing mint Lay the roots in a seed tray and cover with compost.

Shown here on the right are the enlarged buds of blackcurrant which indicate the presence of big bud mite. These buds must be removed.

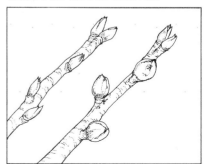

Inside

Here again it is a case of keeping up the continuity of jobs begun earlier. There are likely to be some cuttings which still need potting, and it is advisable to make routine inspections to remove dead and yellowing leaves.

Water carefully and give some ventilation every day if possible.

The gladioli which were lifted early in the autumn should now be thoroughly dry. Remove the stems and place the corms in single layers in boxes so that they can be kept in a cool airy place until planting time.

Start to take cuttings of the perpetual-flowering carnations. Choose non-flowering sideshoots and root in sand in a propagating frame.

Chrysanthemums can be cut back as they finish flowering. Label the best and healthiest plants of each colour to be kept for producing cuttings in the spring, others can be thrown away.

Cyclamen should now be at their best, and the primroses sown in April should be growing well and be in flower at the end of this month or early in January.

Shrubs in pots To provide colour in the unheated greenhouse, it is possible to lift some of the plants from the garden and bring them on to flower early under glass. Keep plenty of soil around the roots and pot carefully. Forsythia, ribes, spiraea, deutzia and lily of the valley will all respond if treated this way.

Bulbs in bowls and pots By now there should be pots and bowls of prepared hyacinths, daffodils, narcissi and tulips to be moved into lighter conditions. I move a few bowls at a time to ensure having a continuity of bulbs in flower. Keep them in a cool light place until the flower buds are showing well before moving

Once the bulb flowers start to grow they may need to be given some form of support. Two methods are shown above.

them into a warm living room, otherwise there is a likelihood of getting either tall leaves and flowers right down in the centre of the bulbs, or bulbs which fail to flower altogether.

In living rooms it is important to keep the bulbs close to a window where they get maximum light. If kept to the back of the room the flowers and leaves will be thin and straggly.

HOUSE PLANTS

Keep plants in the lightest position in the room. The Christmas gift plants such as azaleas, chrysanthemums, flowering bulbs and poinsettias do not like very hot dry conditions, and this may be a cause of failure.

At night, plants should not be left on the windowsill behind drawn curtains as they are likely to be damaged by frost.

Check the rhubarb which is being forced to see if it needs water. Shoots should be ready at the end of this month or in January.

December

Plants of the Month

At this time of the year the garden would look dull and uninteresting were it not for the winter-flowering shrubs and plants and, with careful planning, there should be quite a few of these to choose from. Especially useful are the lovely yellow jasmine, the mahonias, the heathers in many varieties and colours and, of course, the Christmas roses.

TREES

Crataegus (Hawthorn)   Some varieties of this May-flowering tree provide interest at this time of the year in the form of brightly coloured berries. One excellent kind is *C. carrierei* with large scarlet fruits. It grows to around 4·5 or 6 m (15 or 20 ft) in any soil and an open position. Pruning is not necessary.

Ilex (Holly)   The hollies usually grown are varieties of *I. aquifolium*, all of which are undemanding plants for an open or partially shaded position. Many of the varieties have beautifully variegated leaves, and in some instances it would be necessary to grow both male and female forms to get the berries. Recommended are *I. a. argentea marginata* which is the best silver-foliaged holly; Madame Briot with gold-edged leaves—both these grow to 6 m (20 ft)—and Golden King, golden variegated and reaching a height of around 7·5 m (25 ft).

SHRUBS AND CLIMBERS

Cotoneaster   Many of the deciduous and ever-green kinds are particularly valuable for their berries, and the deciduous varieties have the added attraction of autumn-tinted foliage. Suitable for most soils and situations and varying in height *C. conspicuus* Decorus is an evergreen growing to about 1 m (3 ft), with scarlet berries. *C. horizontalis* is deciduous and has a spreading fishbone habit, which is attractive against a wall, red berries and grows to about 1 m (3 ft). *C. salicifolius* Autumn Fire, evergreen, is useful for carpeting the ground as it is only 30 cm (1 ft) tall. Taller growing to 2 m (6 ft) is *C. franchetii*, also evergreen, with silvery foliage and orange scarlet berries.

Erica (Heather)   Coming into flower at this time of the year are the varieties of *Erica carnea*, which will tolerate chalk or lime in the soil. Height from 15 to 45 cm (6 to 18 in). Good varieties include Foxhollow Fairy, pink and white; King

George, deep rose pink; Ruby Glow, dark red and Springwood White and Springwood Pink.

Another species which tolerates chalk, *Erica darleyensis*, comes into flower at much the same time. Growing up to 60 cm (2 ft), this also has a range of good varieties.

Euonymus   Two evergreen shrubs well worth growing for their decorative foliage are *E. japonicus*, or one of its variegated varieties, reaching a height of about 3 m (10 ft), and *E. radicans variegata*, which is much smaller—to about 30 cm (12 in) only—with white-edged leaves that take on a rose-coloured hue in winter. Grow them in ordinary soil and a sunny or shady position. *E. japonicus* makes a good hedge, especially in seaside districts. Trim as necessary in summer but any hard pruning required should be carried out in spring.

Jasmine   The winter jasmine, *Jasminum nudiflorum*, produces bright yellow flowers on slender green shoots throughout the winter months. It makes a good climber, being suited to even a north-facing wall and will eventually reach about 4·5 m (15 ft). Not particular about soil. Prune after flowering, cutting out the shoots

1 Holly with variegated leaves
2 *Erica carnea* Springwood White and *Picea pungens glauca* Procumbens
3 Winter jasmine, *Jasminum nudiflorum*
4 *Helleborus niger*, the Christmas rose
5 Poinsettia, *Euphorbia pulcherrima*

which have just flowered.

Mahonia   Useful evergreen shrubs with holly-like leaves and sprays of yellow flowers, often followed by small purple berries. One of the best forms is *Mahonia japonica* with very fragrant lemon-yellow flowers. It grows to about 2 m (6 ft) and prefers a slightly sheltered position with protection from winds and good soil. No pruning required. Another fine form is Charity, with bright yellow flowers.

BORDER PLANTS

Hellebore   The Christmas rose, *Helleborus niger*, is the first of the hellebores to flower. The white flowers are carried on 30 cm (12 in) stems and will need cloche protection to keep them unmarked if you are intending to cut them for flower arrangements. It grows well in any reasonable soil and a cool, partly shaded place.

VEGETABLES IN THE GARDEN

Jerusalem artichokes, broccoli, Brussels sprouts, cabbage, cauliflower, celery, kale, leeks, lettuce, parsnips, savoy cabbage, swede, turnip.

INSIDE

Flowering Bulbs   For decorating the house this month there should be pots and bowls of hyacinths, if the specially treated ones were planted up in September, and also the beautifully and delicately scented narcissus—varieties such as Paper White and Grand Soleil d'Or.

If possible, these should be kept fairly cool and in the lightest position in the room.

Poinsettia   One of the traditional Christmas flowers, especially in its red form, although there are white and pink kinds as well. Do not allow it to get dry or chilled, and it should continue to be colourful for several months. It can then be discarded. Alternatively, cut back all the shoots to prevent it becoming leggy, and grow on as a most attractive foliage plant.

Solanum (Winter Cherry)   Small shrubby plant with masses of cherry-red fruits which is also popular for Christmas decoration. It can be raised from seed sown in March in a temperature of 15°C(59°F), the seedlings being gradually potted on as required. When in flower in the summer, spray over with water to encourage setting.

Zygocactus (Christmas Cactus) Very decorative plant with pendulous flowers. Water freely when in flower and for a few weeks after flowering. Try not to move plants as this encourages bud drop. Water sparingly. Stand plants in a semi-shaded place outdoors in summer.

115

Vegetable sowing and harvesting chart

	Sow under glass	Sow out of doors	Plant	Depth to sow	Space between rows	Distance to thin/plant
Broad Bean	Feb	Feb-Jul	April	5 cm (2 in)	1 m (3 ft)	15 cm (6 in)
French Bean	Mid-April	Late May	June	2·5 cm (1 in)	45 cm (1½ ft)	20 cm (8 in)
Runner Bean	End-April	Mid-May early June	end May June	5 cm (2 in)	1·5 m (5 ft)	23 cm (9 in)
Beetroot		April-July		2·5 cm (1 in)	38 cm (15 in)	15 cm (6 in)
Leaf Beet		April-July		2·5 cm (1 in)	45 cm (1½ ft)	23 cm (9 in)
Broccoli		Mar-May	Jun-July	1 cm (½ in)	60 cm (2 ft)	45 cm (1½ ft)
Brussels sprouts	Feb	Mar-April	April-Jun	1 cm (½ in)	75 cm (2½ ft)	75 cm (2½ ft)
Cabbage early summer	Feb		Mar-April	1 cm (½ in)	60 cm (2 ft)	45 cm (1½ ft)
summer		Mar-April	April-June	1 cm (½ in)	60 cm (2 ft)	45 cm (1½ ft)
autumn		late-April	June	1 cm (½ in)	60 cm (2 ft)	45 cm (1½ ft)
winter		May	June-July	1 cm (½ in)	60 cm (2 ft)	45 cm (1½ ft)
Savoy		April-May	July-Aug	1 cm (½ in)	60 cm (2 ft)	45 cm (1½ ft)
Cabbage, Spring		Aug	Sept-Oct	1 cm (½ in)	45 cm (1½ ft)	30 cm (1 ft)
Carrots		April-July		0·5 cm (¼ in)	30 cm (1 ft)	10 cm (4 in)
Cauliflower summer	Feb		April	1 cm (½ in)	60 cm (2 ft)	45 cm (1½ ft)
autumn & winter		April-May	June-July	1 cm (½ in)	75 cm (2½ ft)	60 cm (2 ft)
Celery	Mar-April		June		1 m (3 ft)	30 cm (12 in)
Cucumber, Frame	Mar-April		Apr-May	2·5 cm (1 in)		1 m (3 ft)
Ridge	Mid-April	Mid-May	May	2·5 cm (1 in)		1 m (3 ft)
Kale		April-May	July-Aug	1 cm (½ in)	60 cm (2 ft)	60 cm (2 ft)
Leeks	Feb	Mar	June	1 cm (½ in)	38 cm (15 in)	30 cm (12 in)
Lettuce	Feb-Mar Sept-Oct	Mar-Oct		1 cm (½ in)	30 cm (1 ft)	23 cm (9 in)
Marrow	April	May		2·5 cm (1 in)	1 m (3 ft)	60 cm (2 ft)
Onions	Jan	Mar-April Aug-Sept	Mar-Apr	1 cm (½ in)	30 cm (1 ft)	15 cm (6 in)
Parsnips		Mar-May		2·5 cm (1 in)	45 cm (1½ ft)	20 cm (8 in)
Potatoes early			Mar	13 cm (5 in)	60 cm (2 ft)	30 cm (1 ft)
maincrop			April	13 cm (5 in)	75 cm (2½ ft)	45 cm (1½ ft)
Peas	Feb	Mar-June	April	5 cm (2 in)	60 cm-1·5 m (2-5 ft)	8 cm (3 in)
Radish	Feb	Mar-Aug		0·5 cm (¼ in)	23 cm (9 in)	1 cm (½ in)
Spinach		Mar-Sept		2·5 cm (1 in)	30 cm (1 ft)	15 cm (6 in)
Swede		May-June		1 cm (½ in)	30 cm (1 ft)	20 cm (8 in)
Sweet Corn	April	May	May	2·5 cm (1 in)	1 m (3 ft)	38 cm (15 in)
Tomatoes	Mar-April				75 cm (2½ ft)	45 cm (1½ ft)
Turnip		Mar-Sept		1 cm (½ in)	30 cm (1 ft)	15 cm (6 in)

Suggested Varieties	Harvest	
Use Aquadulce for first outdoor sowing, this can be in Nov. in a sheltered area.	June-Oct	Broad Bean
The Prince (for sowing under glass), Masterpiece, Tendergreen.	July-Oct	French Bean
White Achievement, Streamline.	July-Oct	Runner Bean
Boltardy followed by Cheltenham Greentop.	July-Oct	Beetroot
Perpetual Spinach, Swiss Chard.	July-Mar	Leaf Beet
Calabrese followed by White Sprouting and Purple Sprouting.	Sept-May	Broccoli
Peer Gynt, Citadel, Market Rearguard.	Sept-Mar	Brussels sprouts
Hispi, Primo, May Star.	May-June	Cabbage early summer
Greyhound, Winnigstadt.	July-Sept	summer
Market Topper, Autumn Supreme.	Oct	autumn
Christmas Drumhead, Winter White.	Nov-Jan	winter
Ormskirk Late, Rearguard.	Oct-Mar	Savoy
Wheeler's Imperial, April, Offenham.	Apr-June	Cabbage, Spring
Amstel, Scarlet Horn followed by Favourite, then Autumn King.	June-Oct	Carrots
Snowball, Alpha, Dominant, All The Year Round.	June-July	Cauliflower summer
Canberra, Snow's Winter White, St George, Walcheren Winter.	Aug-June	autumn & winter
Solid White, Giant Red.	Oct-Jan	Celery
Improved Telegraph, Femspot.	July-Sept	Cucumber, Frame
Burpee Hybrid.	Aug-Sept	Ridge
Pentland Brigg, Hungry Gap.	Nov-May	Kale
Musselburgh, Prizetaker for sowing under glass.	Sept-Apr	Leeks
Little Gem, Continuity and Webb's Wonderful, then Arctic King and Valdor.	all year	Lettuce
Tender and True, Golden Zucchini, Long Green Trailing.	July-Sept	Marrow
Ailsa Craig followed by Primodoro then Solidity and Express Yellow, Autumn Queen.	June-Sept Feb-June	Onions
Tender and True, Hollow Crown.	Sept-Mar	Parsnips
Homeguard, Foremost, Arran Pilot.	June-July	Potatoes early
Pentland Dell, King Edward VII.	Aug-Oct	maincrop
Feltham First, Little Marvel, Kelvedon Wonder.	June-Oct	Peas
Red Forcing then French Breakfast followed by China Rose for winter cropping.	Apr-Oct	Radish
Greenmarket, Sigmaleaf.	All year	Spinach
Purple Top, Bronze Top, Chignecto.	Oct-Mar	Swede
First of All.	Aug-Oct	Sweet Corn
Alicante, Tangello, The Amateur (for outdoor use only).	July-Oct	Tomatoes
Snowball, then Golden Ball.	June-Mar	Turnip

Glossary

Annual A plant which is raised from seed, flowers and dies within twelve months. Annuals may be divided into different types: those called 'hardy' which can spend their entire lifespan out of doors; the 'half-hardies' which will not survive frost and so must be sown under glass and planted out in early summer, and the 'tender' ones which must be cultivated throughout in a greenhouse.

Bedding A term used for plants which are grown out of doors to give a temporary display of flowers after which they are removed. They may be annual, biennial or perennial. Plants for spring bedding are set out in the autumn, those for summer bedding in late spring or early summer.

Biennial A plant which normally takes two seasons to reach flowering stage, then produces seed and dies. Canterbury bells, honesty and foxgloves are examples of biennial plants.

Blanching The practice of of excluding light from various vegetables at certain stages of their development. It usually improves the flavour by removing the green colouring matter which can impart a bitter taste, and makes the plant more succulent.

Bolting A term used to describe a plant (usually a vegetable) running quickly to seed in dry and warm weather.

Brassica This name is given to all the plants related to the wild cabbage *Brassica oleracea*. All have certain stages in their cultivation in common.

Included under the general term are broccoli, Brussels sprouts, cabbage, cauliflower, kale, swede and turnip.

Buds These are usually of two main kinds, those which give rise to shoots and those which form flowers. The buds on an underground stem such as a potato are known as 'eyes'.

Bulb An underground bud surrounded by fleshy scaley leaves and capable of surviving considerable periods of draught. Examples are tulips, daffodils and hyacinths.

Compost Any mixture of soil, peat, sand and fertilisers in any combination used for potting plants or sowing seeds. The term is also used to describe the decayed remains of garden refuse. Potting and seed-sowing composts are of two main kinds: the John Innes and the peat-based.

Cordon A fruit tree restricted to 1, 2 or 3 stems grown vertically, horizontally, or

Blanching celery.

obliquely at an angle of 45 degrees. Mainly used for apples, pears and gooseberries and especially useful for smaller gardens as they can be planted against walls and fences.

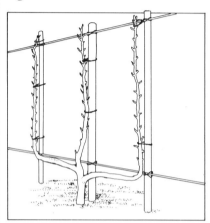

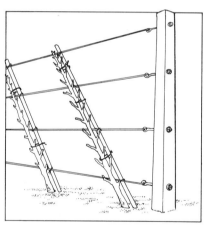

Above Two kinds of cordon.

Corm A short fleshy underground stem with a terminal bud. Often confused with the true bulb.

Crown The junction of the root and stem on hardy border plants from which new growth appears each year.

Cutting A piece of growth cut from a plant for the purpose of producing a similar specimen. Cuttings may be taken from the stems, roots or leaves.

Damping down   A method used to increase the humidity in a greenhouse during warm weather by wetting the floors and staging.

Dead heading   Removing the faded flowers from bulbs and other flowering plants to divert the plant's energies into making more vegetative growth or more flowers instead of producing seed.

Deciduous   A term applied to those trees and shrubs which shed their leaves each autumn.

Disbudding   The thinning out of unwanted growths by removing side buds. Often used when growing chrysanthemums and dahlias to produce one large flower on each stem.

Drill   Seeds are sown in the garden in one of two ways: they are either scattered over the surface of the soil and lightly raked in (broadcast sowing) or they are sown in straight lines in shallow furrows which are drawn out with the corner of a hoe or rake. This is known as sowing in drills. After sowing the soil is replaced and lightly firmed.

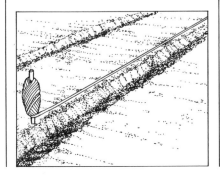

Earthing up   The process of drawing soil up in heaps or ridges around some plants. Celery and leeks are earthed up to blanch their stems, potatoes are earthed up to prevent tubers turning green in the light. Other plants may be earthed up in winter to give the stems support against strong winds.

Evergreen   A plant which retains its leaves throughout the year.

Forcing   A technique of placing plants in a warmer temperature to bring them to maturity earlier than their normal season.

Fumigation   A method of controlling pests and diseases in greenhouses by exposing them to poisonous fumes. For this to be effective the greenhouse must be made as airtight as possible, all doors and ventilators being shut securely. After fumigating, it is advisable to open the door for a period before entering. On no account should conservatories with doors leading into the dwelling house be fumigated as the fumes are likely to find their way into the house. Insecticides and fungicides for this purpose are available in special smoke generators.

Germination   The process of starting seeds into growth. This is affected by three factors: moisture, heat and oxygen; light is rarely necessary. The ability of seeds to germinate readily diminishes with each year they are kept.

Hardening off   In order to prevent a check to the growth of plants by a sudden change in temperature, those plants raised in greenhouses need to be accustomed gradually to outdoor conditions before being planted out in the garden. This is done by moving seedlings first to a garden frame and then to a sheltered place out of doors, see p. 56.

Hardy   A term applied to those plants which are capable of surviving through periods of frost without protection. The 'hardiness' of plants may vary somewhat under the influence of local conditions.

Heeling in   A method of protecting the roots of plants from drying out whilst waiting to be planted. A trench is dug into which the roots are placed with the stems being supported against the side of the trench. The roots are then completely covered with soil. (Page 20).

Humus   The end product from decayed organic matter. It contributes much to the fertility of the soil by increasing the bacterial population and improving its moisture-holding abilities.

Layering   A process by which the plant is encouraged to form roots at a certain point before the new plant is detached from its parent. Some plants, such as strawberries and blackberries layer themselves naturally.

Mulch   A layer of material spread on the surface above the roots of the plant to prevent the soil losing moisture by evaporation and to keep down weeds. Most forms of organic matter can be used as mulches: decayed manure, garden compost, spent hops, mushroom compost, peat or composted tree bark. The mulch should be spread evenly around the plant to a depth of several inches but it must be kept away from the stem. Black polythene and pebbles or gravel can also be used for this purpose.

Naturalise A term used for plants which are grown in as natural a fashion as possible and are left to look after themselves e.g. daffodil bulbs planted in grass.

Perennial Any plant which lives for more than two years. There are two types: the herbaceous perennials which usually die down to ground level each winter and the woody perennials such as the roses, trees and shrubs which do not.

Pinching The process of removing by hand the soft tips of shoots. This encourages the growth of side shoots and the formation of flower buds.

Pricking out The technique of transplanting seedlings from the pots and boxes in which they have sprouted to other boxes or to the soil outside. It results in each seedling having more space in which to grow so that it will make a strong sturdy plant. See page 40.

Rhizome An underground stem which grows horizontally and produces shoots at the tips, e.g. a bearded, or flag, iris.

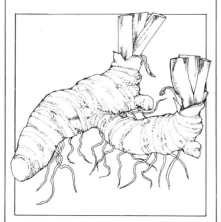

Runner Some plants, such as the strawberry, send out prostrate shoots which form roots at intervals along their length. These are the runners. They provide an easy means of propagation.

Spit The term for a layer of soil as deep as can be conveniently turned on a spade, approximately 25 cm (10 in). Single digging means that the soil is broken up to the depth of a spit.

Spur This has two quite different meanings. It is used to describe the horn-like projections from the base of the petals of aquilegia and delphinium, and is also applied to the close collections of fruit buds found on some fruit trees.

Standard Any plant which is trained with a long bare main stem or trunk carrying a head of branches or shoots on top. Frequently used to describe certain roses and also fruit trees.

Starting A term used to describe the process of bringing into growth any plant which has been dormant or resting. Under natural conditions they would start into growth in their own time but when grown in a greenhouse it may be necessary to simulate those conditions to get them going.

Stool A word used to describe the rootstocks of plants that are easily divided or are capable of throwing up numbers of shoots from the roots, e.g. chrysanthemum, Michaelmas daisy.

Stopping The technique of removing the growing tip of any plant with a view either to preventing its upward growth any further or encouraging it to form side shoots.

Systemic A term applied to many insecticides, fungicides and herbicides which means that the chemical is absorbed into the plant's sap and is carried round within the plant rather than remaining on the surface. It gives the plant a much longer period of protection than a non-systemic control.

Tender Those plants which are not frost hardy and so will not stand a winter in the open are known as tender.

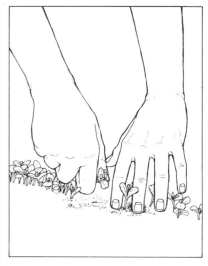

Thinning seedlings

Thinning The operation of removing superfluous seedlings so that those remaining will have sufficient space in which to grow. It should be done as soon as plants are large enough to handle and great care should be taken not to loosen those which are to remain.

Fruit may also be thinned if the trees are carrying over-heavy crops, each cluster being reduced to one or two fruits. Fruit thinning should be delayed until July, by which time any natural thinning should have occurred.

Tilth Soil which has been worked down to a fine crumbly texture is said to have a good tilth. This is essential for successful seed sowing.

Topdressing In order to maintain soil fertility around established plants, fertilisers or other materials such as compost or soil can be applied to the surface of the soil around the plant. Where bulky organic materials are used this is known as mulching. It is important that the soil surface is damp before any topdressing is applied.

Tuber A thickened fleshy root or stem used as a storage organ. Potatoes are examples of stem tubers whilst dahlias are root tubers.

Index

Page numbers in italics refer to illustrations

Acer palmatum, 98, *98*
Achillea, 63
Ageratum, 40, 75
air layering, 41
Allium, 63
Althaea, 75
Alyssum, *15*, 40
  saxatile, 46, 61
Amaryllis, 99
Anemone blanda, 38
  b. White Splendour, *39*
  coronaria, 47
  japonica, 90, *90*
  planting, 88
annuals, 118
  half-hardy, 40, 48, 52
  hardy, 36, 43, 44, 72
  sowing, 61, 92
  stopping, 101
Antirrhinum, 40, 82
apples: picking, 88–9
  storing, 100
apple trees: feeding, 29
  pruning, 84, *84*, 108, *108*
  spraying, 53
  thinning fruits, 73
Arabis, 46
Aster, 40, 98, *98*
Aubrieta, 46, 61
Azalea, 23, 34, 60, 95, 113

beans, broad: planting, 37
  removing tips, 64
  sowing, 28, 32, 36, 45, 53, 108
  spraying, 81
beans, French: sowing, 53
  spraying, 64
beans, runner: feeding, 73, 81
  preparing ground, 53
  sowing, 53, 56, 64
  spraying, 64–5
bedding plants, 51, 118
  hardening off, 56, *56*
  planting, 60, *60*
  watering, 60
beet, leaf, 45, 53, 64, 73
beetroot, 37, 45, 73, 88, 100
Begonia, 75
  feeding, 57, 76
  overwintering, 24–5
  potting, 40, 68
  resting, 92, 101
  semperflorens: planting out, 57
  sowing, 32, 40
  staking, 68

starting, 32
  topdressing, 48
Bellis, 61, 96
Berberis, 46, 106
Bergenia, 30
  Ballawley, *31*
biennials, 52, 61, 72, 118
big bud mite, 45, 112, *112*
birds, 27, 29, 43
blackberries, 14, 65, 73, 89
blackcurrants: bug bud mite, 45, 112, *112*
  cuttings, 108
  feeding, 29, 45
  planting distances, 14
  pruning, 29, 84, *84*
  spraying, 45, 89
blanching, 118, *118*
blossom end rot, 69
bolting, 118
botrytis, 24
brassicas, 118
broccoli, 29, 45, 53, 88
Broom, 52
Browallia, 40, 83
Brussels sprouts: feeding, 81, 100
  picking, 112
  planting, 45, 53, 64
  sowing, 32, 36
  spraying, 88
Buddleia, 28, 82
buds, 118
bulbs, 86, 118
  Christmas flowering, 85
  heeling in, 52
  naturalising, 96, 120
  planting, 86, 88, *89*, 96
  planting depths, 89
  in pots, 109, 113
  potting, 92, *93*
  removing dead flowers, 44
  staking, *113*

cabbage: feeding, 29, 100
  planting, 45, 53, 100, *100*
  sowing, 32, 36, 45, 53, 81
  spraying, 88
cabbage root fly, 73
Calceolaria, 47, *47*
  potting, 85, 101
  pricking out, 68
  sowing, 40, 57
Calendula, 75
Calluna, 82
Camellia japonica, 31
Campanula (Canterbury Bells), 61, 96
  medium, *62*, 63
Candytuft, 61
canker, 21, *21*

Canterbury Bells, 61, *62*, 63, 96
Carnation, 47
  annual: sowing, 40
  cuttings, 25, 32, 113
  housing, 92
  layering, *72*
  planting, 80
  potting, 68
  staking, 57
  stopping, 76
Carpenteria, 74
carrot fly, 73
carrots: lifting, 100
  sowing, 37, 45, 53, 64, 73
  storing, 88
Caryopteris, 28, 90
cauliflower: feeding, 29
  planting, 45, 53
  protecting, 20, 65, 112
  sowing, 32, 36, 45
  spraying, 88
Ceanothus, 28, 54, 82
celery: blanching, *118*
  earthing up, 81, 88, 100
  feeding, 64
  hardening off, 56
  planting, 53, 64, *64*
  sowing, 40
Cerastium, 63
Chaenomeles, 38
  speciosa, *38*
Cheiranthus, *see* Wallflower
chemicals: required, 13
  time to use, 16
  types available, 16–17
  use, 15–16
cherry, 14
  ornamental, 54, *54*, 98, 107
  spraying, 65
Chimonanthus fragrans, 22
Chinese cabbage, 73
Chionodoxa, 31, 92, 96
chives, 28
Chrysanthemum, 107
  annual: sowing, 61
  cutting down, 113
  cuttings, 32, *32*, 40
  disbudding, 80, *80*
  feeding, 72, 92, 109
  in frame, 40
  hardening off, 48
  in house, 113
  housing, 92
  lifting, 97
  maximum, 82
  outdoor: preparing ground, 44
  planting, 52, *52*
  potting, 68, *68*
  pinching out, 48
  protecting, 88

removing side shoots, 101
spraying, 68, 92
staking, 92
stock plants, 25
stopping, *52, 61, 76, 85*
topdressing, 85
Cineraria, 23, *23*
feeding, 109
pests, 101
pricking out, 68
potting, 76, 85
sowing, 40, 57
watering, 101
Cissus, 33
Cistus, 62
purpureus, 62
Clarkia, 61
Clematis, 46, 54, 74
pruning, 28, 36, 52, 72
soil for, 95
climbers, 72, 88
cloches, 28
club root, 45, 64
Colchicum, 80, 99
autumnale, 99
Coleus, 83
composts, 17, 118
compost heap, 88, 104
conifers: planting, 44, 96, 104, *105*
protecting, 102
wind damage, 27
conservatory, 17
containers: planting, 60, 96
Convallaria, *see* Lily of the Valley
cordons, 118, *118*
corms, 118
Cornus, 22, 30
Cortaderia, 98, *99*
Corylopsis, 30
Corylus, 30
Cosmos, 82, *82*
Cotoneaster, 114
Cotinus, 98
courgettes, 48, 53, 56, 64, 73
Crataegus, 114
Crocosmia Spitfire, *91*
Crocus, 20, 23, 30, 96
in pots, 92
crop rotation, *21*
crown, 118
cucumber: feeding, 68, 73, 77
flavour, 77
flowers, *57*, 73
hardening off, 56
picking, 85
pinching out, 68, 73
planting, 57, *57*, 64
sowing, 48, 53
topdressing, 68
cuttings, 118
half-ripe, 76, *76*
hardwood, 96, *96*
softwood, *48*
Cyclamen, 91, 107, *107*
dew on, 92
drying off, 57
housing, 92
planting, 80

potting, 68
removing buds, 76, 101
sowing, 68, 85
starting, 76
Cydonia, *see* Chaenomeles

Daffodil, *see* Narcissus
Dahlia, 90
cutting down, 97
cuttings, 40
disbudding, 80
feeding, 72
Goody Goody, *90*
planting, 53
preparing for cuttings, 24, *25*
staking, 72
stopping, 61
storing, 97
damping down, 119, *119*
Daphne mezereum, 14, 30, *30*
dead heading, 119
Delphinium, 52, 61, 75, *83*
Deutzia, 113
Dianthus (Pink), 63, 75
cutting back, 61
cuttings, 76
Doris, *74*
planting, 80
soil for, 95
Digitalis, *see* Foxglove
digging, 13, 20, 102, 108
Dimorphotheca, 82
aurantiaca, 82
disbudding, 119
division, 28
Doronicum, *14*, 46

earthing up, 119
earwigs, 80
Elaeagnus pungens maculata, 30, *30*
Eranthis, 23
Erica, 44, 90, 114
carnea Springwood White, *114*
Erigeron, 82
Erythronium, 31
Escallonia, 52, 62
Eschscholzia, 61, 75
Euonymus, 114
Euphorbia, 55
Exacum, 99

fertilisers, 13
forcing, 119
Forget-me-not, 47, *47*, 61, 96
Forsythia, 38, *38*, 44, 113
Foxglove, 55, *55*, 61, 96
frame, *16*, 17
Fritillaria, 47, 96
fruit: picking, *89*
storing, 100, *100*
fruit trees, 14–15
in containers, 14–15
grease bands, 89
planting, 37, 108
planting distances, 14

pollination, 14
pruning, 20, 112
rootstocks, 14
spraying, 21, 112
Fuchsia, 90
cuttings, 33, 92
feeding, 57
potting, 25, 32–3, 40–1, 48–9, 57, 101, 109
pruning, 28
removing buds, 109
resting, 101
starting, 33
watering, 57
fumigation, 119
fungicides: use, 15–16

Galanthus (Snowdrop), *22*, 23, 96
garden: from scratch, 11–12
Garrya, 22
elliptica, 22
Genista, 54
Geranium: hardy, 55
tender, *see* Pelargonium
Geum, 90
Gladiolus, 83, *83*
lifting, 88
planting, 44
staking, 61
storing, 113
glossary, 118–20
Gloxinia, 75, *75*
overwintering, 24–5
potting, 40, 68
resting, 92, 101
sowing, 32, 40
starting, 32
Godetia, 61
gooseberries: cuttings, 100
feeding, 29, 45
planting distances, 14
pruning, 29, *29*
spraying, 45, 65
grass: for whole garden at first, 11
grease bands, 89
greenhouse, *16*, 17
damping down, 68
heating, 109
insulating, 27
shading, 56, 68, *69*, 92
ventilating, 40, 48, *69*, 76, 101
washing down, 24
watering, 76, 77
Gunnera, 104

Hamamelis mollis, 30, *31*
hanging baskets, *41*, 57, 60–1
hardening off, 56, *56*, 119
Hebe, 44, 82
hedge: planting, *105*
pruning, 78, *81*
Rose, 67
heeling in, 20, *20*, 119
Helenium, 83, *83*
Helianthemum, 54, 61
Helianthus, 91

Helleborus niger, 111, 115, *115*
herbs, 45, 81
Hibiscus, 82
Holly, 111, 114, *114*
Honeysuckle, 22, 60, *62*
house plants: cleaning leaves, 25
    cuttings, 85, *85*
    feeding, 77
    housing, 92
    humidity for, 101, *101*
    potting, 49, *49*
    removing to greenhouse, 25
    spraying, 69, 92
    standing outdoors, 69
humus, 13, 119
Hyacinth, 85, 92, 101
Hydrangea, 28, 74
Hypericum, 74
    Rowallane, *74*

Ilex (Holly), 111, 114, *114*
insecticides: use, 15–16
Iris, 23
    bearded, 61, *61*, 63
    reticulata, *23*, 96
Ivy: cuttings, 33

Jasminum nudiflorum, 114, *115*
    pruning, 28
Jerusalem artichokes, 20, 29, 37, 108
Juniper, 106

Laburnum, 54
    watereri vossii, *54*
Lathyrus, *see* Sweet Pea
Lavatera, 83
Lavender, 74, 80
    Hidcote, *74*
lawn: after bulbs cut down, 73
    edging, 36
    feeding, 36, 44
    forking, 105, *105*
    fungus, 70
    moss, 28, 36
    mowing, 36, 43, 44, 53, 64, 88
    preparing for turfing, 20
    raking, 28, 97
    sowing, 36, 44, *45*, 88
    spiking, 105
    sweeping, 112
    topdressing, 105
    turfing, 28, *29*, 97
    weeds, 53, 81
lawn mowers, 44, 105
layering, 41, 119
leaf miner, 101
leeks, 32, 56, 64, *64*, 88
lettuce: planting, 37, 45, 100
    sowing, 32, 36, 45, 64, 73, 81, 88
Leucojum, 39, 91
Lilac, 60, 62–3
Lilium (Lily), 80, 83, 104, *104*, 112
    regale, *83*
Lily of the Valley, 28, 55, 113
liming, 20

Liquidambar, 98
Lobelia, 15, 40
loganberries, 14, 65, 73, 89
Lonicera (Honeysuckle), 22, 60
    americana, *62*
Lupin, 52, 61, 63

Magnolia, 46
    soulangiana, *46*
Mahonia, 114–15
Malus, 46
Marigold, 40
Marrow, 48, 53, 56, 64, 73
Metasequoia, 98
Michaelmas Daisy, 98, *98*
mint, 28, 112, *112*
Montbretia, 91
mulching, 58, 119
Muscari, *14*, 47, 88
Myosotis, see Forget-me-not

Narcissus (incl. Daffodil):
    cutting back leaves, 61
    planting, 88, 96
    in pots, 85, 92, 101
narcissus fly, 52
Nasturtium, 61, 75
naturalising, 96, 120
nectarines, 14
Nemesia, 40
Nerine, 99
Nicotiana, 40
nitrogen, 13
Nymphaea, 74, 75

onion fly, 73
onions: feeding, 73
    lifting, 88
    planting, 29, 45
    ripening, 81
    sowing, 24, 36, 45, 81, 88

Paeonia, 55
    officinalis, *55*
Pampas grass, 98, *99*
Pansy, 36, 76, 80, 96
Papaver (Poppy), 61, 63
    nudicaule, *63*
Parsley, 45
parsnips, 36, 45, 53
Parthenocissus, 98
peaches, 14
pears, 45, 100
peas: planting, 37, 45
    sowing, 32, 36, 45, 53, 64, 108
Pelargonium (Geranium): cuttings, 57,
    76, 85, 92
    feeding, 57
    potting, 32–3, 40–1, 92, 101, 109
    Regal, 55
    removing buds, 109
    watering, 57
    Zonal, *15*, 63
perennials, hardy: cuttings, 44

    dividing, 28, 36, 95, 97
    feeding, 28, 44
    planting, 95
    staking, 52
    thinning, 44, 52
Pernettya, 106
Petunia, 40, 75
Philadelphus, 62
Philodendron, 33
Phlomis, 74
Phlox, 40, 61, 75
phosphorus, 13
Physalis, 107
Picea pungens glauca Procumbens, *114*
    p. Kosteri, 106, *106*
Pieris formosa Forrestii, 38, *39*
pinching out, 120
Pink, *see* Dianthus
plums, 65, 73, 89
Poinsettia, 113, 115, *115*
pollination, 14
Polyanthus, 52, 96
Poppy, 61, 63
potash, 13
potatoes: chitting, 25, *25*
    early, 37
    earthing up, 53, 65
    planting, 37, 45
    storing, 100
Potentilla, 28, 62
pot plants: feeding, 76
pricking out, *40*, 48, 120
Primula, 31, 39, 46–7
    feeding, 92
    obconica, 107, *107*
    planting, 72
    potting, 77, 85, 101
    protecting buds, 20
    removing buds, 101
    sowing, 40, 68
propagating frame, 24, *24*
Prunus 54, *54*, 98, 107
Pulmonaria, 23
Pyracantha, 107
    rogersiana Flava, *106*

radish, 36, 45, 64, 73
raspberries: feeding, 29, 45
    planting distances, 14
    pruning, 29, 84, *84*
    spraying, 45, 65, 73, 89
    thinning, 53
red currants, 108, *108*
Red Hot Poker, 104
rhizomes, 120, *120*
Rhododendron, 54
    cutting into shape, 60
    dead heading, 60
    planting, 34
    praecox, 38
    soil for, 95
Rhoicissus, 33
rhubarb: flowers, 65
    forcing, 20, 25, 108, *113*
    planting, 28
Rhus typhina, 98
Ribes, 38, 44, 113

Robinia, 62
rock garden, 28, 44, 97, *97*
rock plants: cuttings, 72
   planting, 80–1, 95
   shearing over, 61, *61*
rock wall, *47*
rootstocks, 14
Rosa (Rose) Albertine, *67*
   canina Andersonii, *67*
   dead heading, 72, 88
   diseases, 58
   feeding, 36
   Grandpa Dickson, *66*
   hedge, 67
   mulching, 36
   pests, 58
   planting, 34, 104, 112
   planting for effect, 67
   pruning, 28, 80, *80*, 104, 112
   Roseraie de l'Hay, *66*
   rugosa, *67*
   scented, 66–7
   spraying, 36, 52
   suckers, 60, *60*
   types, 66
rotary cultivator, 112
Rubber plant, 41
Rudbeckia, 91
   Marmalade, *91*
runners, 120

Sage, 28
Saintpaulia, 99, *99*
Salix alba, 22–3
Salpiglossis, 40, 85
Salvia, 40
Saxifraga, 39
Schizanthus, 33, 41, 55, 85, 101
Scilla, 39, *39*, 88, 92
Sedum, 91
   Autumn Joy, *67*
   telephium, *91*
seed bed, 36–7, *37*
seedlings: pricking out, *40*, 48, 120
seeds: germination, 119
   sowing, 33, 119, *119*
   storing, 18
shallots, 37

shrubs: cuttings, 48, *48*, 76, *76*, 85,
   96, *96*
   cuttings: potting up, 85
   feeding, 36
   planting, 20, 34, 95, 104, 112
   in pots, 113
   pruning, 20, 28, 36, 44, 52, 60, 72
   suckers, 20
silver leaf disease, 73
site clearing, 10
Skimmia, 107
slugs, 43
snow, 18
Snowdrop, 22, 23, 96
soil, 12–13
Solanum, 115
Solidago, 91
spinach, 45, 53, 64, 81
Spiraea, 46, 76
spraying, 60
spur, 120
starting, 120
Stocks: Beauty of Nice, 85, 101
   Brompton, 76, 85
   East Lothian, 85, 101
   Night-scented, 61
   Ten-week, 40
stool, 120
stopping, 120
strawberries: feeding, 29, 45
   layering, *73*
   planting distances, 14
   protecting, 53, 65
   runners, 84
   spraying, 45, 73, 89
   under cloches, 45
Streptocarpus, 32, 40, 63
suckers: removal, 20
swede, 53, 100
sweet corn, 48, 53, 56, 64, 88
Sweet Pea, 75
   care, 72
   hardening off, 40
   planting out, 44
   sowing, 24
   stopping, 32
Sweet William, 61, 63, 96
Syringa (Lilac), 60, 62–3

Tamarix, 90
tar oil wash, 21
thinning, 120, *120*
Thuja occidentalis Rheingold, 106, *106*
Thyme, 28
times: in different parts of country, 10
tomatoes: feeding, 48, 69, 73, 85
   greenback, 77
   planting, 40, 48, 53
   removing leaves, 77, 85, 88
   removing side shoots, 68–9, *69*
   sowing, 32, 40, 48
   watering, 69, 85
tools, *12*
topdressing, 120
Tradescantia, 107
trees: planting, 20, 34, 95, 104, 112
   pruning, 20
   suckers, 20
Tropaeolum, *see* Nasturtium
tubers, 120
Tulip, 47, 96, 101
turnips, 53, 64, 81, 100

vegetable garden, *63*
vegetables, 13–14
   harvesting chart, 116–17
   sowing chart, 116–17
Verbascum, 83
Viburnum, 23
   bodnantense, *22*
Viola, 30, 36

Wallflower, 46, 47, 61, 96
watering, 24, 56, 58, *65*
   capillary bench, *75*
Water Lily, 74, *75*
weeds, 44, 52, 70
Weigela, 52, 54
white currants, 108, *108*
whitefly, 68
Wisteria, 55

Zinnia, 40
Zygocactus, 115

List of chemicals and suppliers

Boots Garden Chemicals

This list gives the range of Boots Garden Chemicals at time of going to press. The full range is available from larger Boots branches

Ant Destroyer
Calomel Dust
Derris Dust
Garden Fertiliser
Garden Insect Killer
Garden Insect Powder
Greenfly Killer
Hormone Rooting Powder
Lawn Fertiliser and Weedkiller
Lawn Reviver
Lawn Weed and Feed
Liquid Fertiliser
Lawn Weedkiller
Moss Killer and Fertiliser
Nettle Killer
Pot Plant Food
Rose Fertiliser (Liquid)
Rose Fertiliser (Granular)
Slug Destroyer
Sodium Chlorate Weedkiller
Systemic Greenfly Killer
Tomato Fertiliser
Warfarin Bait
Potting Compost
Seed & Cutting Compost

Suppliers

Seed houses
Asmer Seeds Ltd., Asmer House, Ash Street, Leicester
Thomas Butcher Ltd., 60 Wickham Road, Shirley, Croydon, Surrey
Samuel Dobie & Son Ltd., Upper Dee Mills, Llangollen, Clwyd
Hurst, Gunson, Cooper Taber Ltd., Witham, Essex
Sutton & Sons Ltd., Hele Road, Torquay, Devon
W. J. Unwin Ltd., Histon, Cambridge

Fruit
Blackmoor Nurseries, Liss, Hampshire
Ken Muir, Honeypot Farm, Weeley Heath, Clacton-on-Sea, Essex
Thomas Rivers & Son Ltd., The Nurseries, Sawbridgeworth, Hertfordshire
Scotts Nurseries (Merriott) Ltd., Merriott, Somerset

Shrubs and trees
Hillier & Sons, Winchester, Hampshire
Notcutts Nurseries Ltd., Woodbridge, Suffolk
L. R. Russell, Windlesham, Surrey

Herbaceous plants
Bressingham Gardens, Diss, Norfolk
Thomas Carlile, Twyford, Reading, Berkshire
Unusual Plants, Beth Chatto, White Barn House, Elmstead Market, Colchester, Essex

Bulbs
Walter Blom & Son Ltd., Coombelands Nurseries, Leavesden, Watford, Hertfordshire
Broadleigh Gardens, Barr House, Bishop's Hull, Taunton, Somerset
Van Tubergen, Willowbank Wharf, Ranelagh Gardens, London SW6 3JY

Roses
Cants of Colchester Ltd., Mile End, Colchester, Essex
C. Gregory & Son Ltd., Toton Lane, Stapleford, Nottingham
R. Harkness & Co. Ltd., Hitchen, Hertfordshire
Murrells of Shrewsbury, Portland Nurseries, Shrewsbury

Water Gardens, plants and accessories
Highlands Water Gardens, Rickmansworth, Hertfordshire
Lotus Water Garden Products Ltd., Chesham, Buckinghamshire
Stapeley Water Gardens Ltd., London Road, Stapeley, Nantwich, Cheshire

Greenhouses and frames
Alitex Ltd., Station Road, Alton, Hampshire
Alton Glasshouses Ltd., P.O. Box 3, Bewdley, Worcestershire
Crittall Warmlife Ltd., Crittall Road, Witham, Essex
Edenlite Ltd., Hawksworth, Swindon, Wiltshire
Marley Greenhouses Ltd., Storrington, Sussex
Tropical Greenhouses, 14 Sanderson St., Sheffield